On The Rampage
Corporate Power and the Destruction of Democracy

Russell Mokhiber &
Robert Weissman

Common Courage Press   Monroe, Maine

Copyright © 2005 by Russell Mokhiber &
Robert Weissman
All rights reserved.
Cover design by Matt Wuerker
and Erica Bjerning
Cartoons by Oliphant, reprinted by permission of
Amuniversal

ISBN: 1-56751-214-3 paper
ISBN 1-56751-215-1 cloth

**Library of Congress Cataloging-in-Publication Data is
available on request from the publisher**

Common Courage Press
121 Red Barn Road
Monroe, ME 04951

800-497-3207

FAX (207) 525-3068
orders-info@commoncouragepress.com

See our website for more about this book.
www.commoncouragepress.com

First Printing
Printed in Canada

Contents

Part Three: Global Domination

Part Four: The Corporatist Octopus

Introduction

More than six years ago, we decided to call a weekly column that we were planning to launch "Focus on the Corporation." A conservative group gaining prominence went by the name Focus on the Family, and it seemed to us that news coverage and political discussion of social, economic and political problems focused on just about everything but the corporation.

That seemed upside down to us. As longtime editors of *Corporate Crime Reporter* (Russell) and *Multinational Monitor* (Robert), we have come to believe that corporations are the driving force in the political economy, as well as the primary shaper of the prevailing culture.

Many of the social problems that are frequently the subject of attention—crime and violence, welfare dependency, erosion of values, unresponsive government—we thought, and think, can be traced in significant part to abuse of corporate power. For example, corporate crime and violence, we knew, inflicts far more damage on society, whether measured in dollars or lives, than street crime.

And then there are the many problems that we too infrequently hear about: the re-colonization of the developing countries, the contamination of our food supply with pesticides and genetically engineered organisms, the routine denial of the legalized guaranteed right to organize in the United States, not to mention the Third World.

These problems, and many more, result from concentrated corporate power.

As we highlight varied corporate abuses, and citizen resistance, in our columns, we have tried to draw attention to the corporation as an institution, with unique powers, motivations and attributes. Although the law often treats corporations as if they were actual human beings, and despite corporate efforts to portray themselves as part of the community (every community), corporations are fundamentally different than you and me. For example:

- Corporations have perpetual life.
- Corporations can be in two or more places at the same time.
- Corporations cannot be jailed.
- Corporations have no conscience or sense of shame.
- Corporations pursue a single-minded goal, profit, and are typically legally prohibited from seeking other ends.
- There are no limits, natural or otherwise, to corporations' potential size.
- Because of their political power, they are able to define or at very least substantially affect, the civil and criminal regulations that define the boundaries of permissible behavior. Virtually no individual criminal has such abilities.
- Corporations can combine with each other, into bigger and more powerful entities.

These unique attributes—which we explore further in the Corporatist Octopus—give corporations extraordinary power, and makes the challenge of checking their power all the more difficult. The institutions are much more powerful than individuals, which makes all the more frightening their single-minded profit-maximizing efforts. Compounding the problem, many of the sanctions we impose on individuals—not just imprisonment, but the more important social norms of shame and community disapproval—have limited relevance to or impact on corporations.

This book is a selection of columns we have written over the last five years. It is organized into nine thematic sections that contain snapshots of important moments or topics. The Criminal Element discusses the corporate crime wave sweeping the United States. Beltway Bandits and Welfare Cheats identifies the fruits of corporate political influence—tax breaks, giveaways and other gifts. The Corporatist Octopus includes dispatches on rampant commercialism and corporate claims to constitutional rights. Global Domination shines a light on corporate globalization. Fronting for Big Business examines both pure corporate front groups and growing alliances between nonprofits and corporations. Labor looks at the corporate onslaught against working people. The Insanity Defense challenges militarism and the Bush administration wars. The Worst highlights *Multinational Monitor*'s annual feature, the Ten Worst Corporations of the year. Resistance shows that, while corporations are sabotaging our democracy, poisoning the planet, ripping off consumers and suppressing workers, more and more people are standing up, and organizing themselves to take back control of our societies.

Our columns are published regularly in *The Progressive Populist* and *Eat the State*, an alternative weekly in Seattle, and on-line by Common Dreams, Znet and others. They appear occasionally in newspapers across the country, Third World Network's syndication service and magazines, newsletters, journals, zines and on-line publications throughout the world.

We also distribute the column through an e-mail service, and we've been heartened by a group of thousands of on-line subscribers that is constantly expanding and prepared to challenge our assumptions, claims and proposals. You too can sign up to receive the columns—roughly one a week, with virtually no other postings—at http://lists.essential.org/mailman/listinfo/corp.focus or by sending an e-mail message to corp-focus-request@lists.essential.org with the text: subscribe. And you can check out previous columns at www.corporatepredators.org.

PART ONE

THE CRIMINAL ELEMENT

Get tough on crime. More money for crime fighting. Put more cops on the streets. These calls, by now political cliche, are the stuff of modern-day politics in the United States.

Virtually never, however, do the politicians puffing these bromides mean that the nation should get tough on corporate crime, that more money should be made available to the staggeringly underfunded corporate crime police in the Justice Department, the Federal Trade Commission, the Food and Drug Administration and other corporate crime-fighting federal agencies, or that the Occupational Safety and Health Administration or the Department of Agriculture need more inspectors to crack down on corporations endangering their employees through unsafe workplaces or imperiling consumers by selling them dirty food.

Politicians and the media alike are blind to the corporate crime wave, even though corporate crime and violence inflicts far more damage on society—whether measured in dollars or lives—than street crime, horrible though the toll of street crime may be. While there are approximately 20,000 homicides in the United States attributed to street crime a year, air pollution takes more than 50,000 lives a year in the United States and an even greater number die annually from workplace-related disease. Burglary and robbery cost victims approximately $3 billion a year, while healthcare fraud takes more than $100 billion from taxpayers and consumers.

Deterring corporate crime and violence requires beefing up the governmental enforcement agencies, and much more. Among other measures, it requires criminal penalties and jail time for corporate executives who oversee corporate violence, preserving the civil justice system, and especially the award of punitive damages against wrongdoers, and depriving contracts and government awards to corporations which break the law. Above all, it will require a cultural shift, so that our society treats corporate violence and wrongdoing with the gravity now reserved for street crime.

Really Mean and Really Stupid: Exxon Funds Attacks on Punitive Damages

February 19, 1999

On March 23, 1989, the Exxon Valdez, one of Exxon's largest oil tankers, under the command of a captain who had been drinking and who abandoned the bridge, struck a reef and spilled eleven million gallons of crude oil into the Prince William Sound in Alaska.

In September 1994, an Alaska jury found Exxon liable for punitive damages for its conduct in causing the oil spill and assessed $5 billion against the company. The lawsuit was brought by commercial fishermen, Alaska natives and others directly harmed by the spill.

In the nearly five years since its jury verdict, Exxon has not paid a penny of the damages. Instead, it has chosen to use an appeals process to delay and possibly defeat any payment.

To commemorate the Exxon Valdez oil spill, the world's largest oil company has decided to ratchet up the corporate attack on punitive damages.

It has just come to our attention that last year, Exxon funded Harvard Law Professor W. Kip Viscusi to look into the issue of punitive damages. Viscusi obliged, and wrote an article for the *Georgetown Law Journal* advocating the abolition of punitive damages. ("The Social Costs of Punitive Damages Against Corporations in Environmental and Safety Torts," by W. Kip Viscusi, 87 *Georgetown Law Journal* 2(285), November 1998.)

In a footnote to the article, Viscusi discloses that the research for the article was funded in part by "a grant from the Exxon Corporation."

But as a short conversation we had with Viscusi made clear, the Harvard Professor doesn't want the world to know how much Exxon paid him.

To begin the conversation, we asked how much money he received from Exxon, Viscusi's first reply: "I don't even know."

"I have several projects," Viscusi said. "This is one paper I did, but I'm working on several other things."

Well, how much did you receive in total from Exxon?

"I don't remember that either," Viscusi replied.

When asked whether he received more than one check from Exxon, Viscusi responds: "Yes, but it was for different projects that overlap the time period."

When asked whether he can give a ballpark figure of how much money he took from Exxon, Viscusi says "no," arguing that the information is not public information.

Viscusi says the he received money from Exxon just in 1998.

Finally, when pressed again as to why he won't reveal the amount of money he took from Exxon for the research on punitive damages, Viscusi responds bluntly—"It's none of your business."

We disagree. It makes a difference whether Viscusi took $10 or $10,000 or $100,000 from Exxon. As readers we have a right to know.

But we also agree with Georgetown Professor David Luban who applauds Viscusi for disclosing the fact of Exxon's funding in an age when other academics do not. We also agree that "when one learns that an interested party has funded work, there should be a higher threshold of critical examination." And Viscusi's Exxon funded work doesn't withstand the higher threshold of critical examination.

Luban, a professor of law and philosophy, wrote a rebuttal to Viscusi's article in the same issue of the Georgetown Law Journal.

In "A Flawed Case Against Punitive Damages," 82 *Georgetown Law Journal* 2(359) (November 1998), Luban dissects Viscusi's argument, finding "thirteen critical errors that if

I'm right, undermine Viscusi's argument at every stage."

In a nutshell, Viscusi argues that punitive damages don't create social benefits, and they do impose social costs on businesses, and thus should be eliminated.

To show that punitive damages create no social benefits, Viscusi argues that accident rates in environmental and other cases are not statistically significantly different in the four states that don't have punitive damages (Michigan, Nebraska, New Hampshire, and Washington) than the 46 states that do.

Luban says that he disagrees that the lack of difference between the four no-punitive-damages states and the other 46 shows that punitive damages are ineffective.

"Even if a business is in one of those four states, they won't look only to those states' tort regimes," Luban says. "They will look at any state that they might be sued in. After all, there are relatively few businesses that are strongly local in the sense that they operate locally, all of their customers are local, and their safety procedures and equipment are local."

And Luban argues that punitive damages are not there simply to deter all forms of unsafe conduct. Punitive damages are meant to be awarded only when the defendant's conduct has been egregious. Justice Richard Neely of West Virginia has put forward a useful formula in TXO v. Alliance Resources, 1992: punitive damages exist to punish defendants whose conduct is either "really mean" or "really stupid." And as a result, they are not awarded very often.

Viscusi argues that punitive damage judgments are "out of control." But Luban says that on average, about three percent of plaintiffs' jury victories end with punitive damages being awarded against the defendants.

How can it be, we asked, that two scholars looking at the same data come to such radically different conclusions.

"Observers of the punitive damages scene focus on different aspects," Luban says. "Those of us who don't think punitive damages are out of control tend to look at the low overall incidence of punitive damages and the relatively low median of punitive damages—about $50,000. What critics look at is the relatively high mean—the average—which is $735,000."

When you have a high mean and a low median, it shows that you have a whole population of relatively low punitive damages with a few, very, very high punitive awards that bring the average up, Luban says.

Punitive damages are a retributive sanction: they send a message to corporate America that what you have done is wrong and intolerable in a civil society.

Exxon's behavior in Prince William Sound was either really mean or really stupid and is deserving of punishment. Instead of attacking punitive damages, it should focus on cleaning up its act to ensure that the nightmare of Valdez will not be repeated.

Electronic Ankle Bracelets, Anyone?

September 20, 1999

Can it be any more clear that the national response to the corporate crime wave sweeping the country has been an utter and abysmal failure?

This is to take nothing away from the hard-working prosecutors who bust their chops working day in and day out, with minimal resources, dodging political attacks from the corporate lobbyists whose primary job it is to keep the cops on their heels and off their case.

For example, lack of enforcement of federal worker safety laws by Clinton administration has resulted in fewer inspections and fewer violations cited compared to prior administrations. Whose fault is that? Not the head of the Occupational Safety and Health Administration, who claims in his defense that for him to do an adequate job, his meager $350 million budget, which is constantly under attack by the corporate crime lobby, would have to be bumped up to at least $7 billion.

Same with antitrust enforcement. Between 1977 and 1997, the total budgets of the two primary antitrust enforcement agencies—the Federal Trade Commission and the Justice Department's Antitrust Division decreased by 7 percent in constant dollars while the GNP grew by 112 percent. Mergers have increased by 550 percent since 1992.

According to Albert Foer, director of the American Antitrust Institute, the failure of antitrust enforcement has resulted in airlines that monopolize hub terminals, international cartels that cost consumers dearly, price fixing and bid rigging that are a continual abuse of the system, monopolies that can control the global flow of information, and agricultural, meatpacking and food retailing industries that are unduly concentrated.

Even when the system works, and the prosecutors nail the criminals to the wall, what good does it do? The recent criminal convictions of major corporations for fixing the prices of vitamins in the United States resulted in two of the biggest criminal fines in the history of corporate crime.

Earlier this year, Hoffman LaRoche pled guilty and was fined $500 million and BASF pled guilty and was fined $225 million for leading a worldwide conspiracy to raise and fix prices and allocate market shares for certain vitamins sold in the United States and elsewhere.

Hoffman LaRoche and BASF alone control 80 percent of the vitamin market worldwide. What impact did the fines have on the behavior of these two criminals? It made them more aggressive in their desire to control the remaining 20 percent of the market.

That's according to Eugene Reed, the Arkansas broker who first blew the whistle on the price fixing conspiracy.

"They have become super aggressive and more committed (since their convictions)," Reed told us earlier this month. "They are already at the foot of the bridge. They sent signals into the marketplace. They want to drive all other vitamin suppliers out of the world market and control it themselves."

The lesson: even the largest criminal fines ever levied in the United States were too small to affect giant multinational corporations.

When individuals commit street crimes, on the other hand, they pay the price with a loss of freedom. That's why by next year, there will be two million inmates in U.S. prisons and jails and the United States will overtake Russia as the world leader in the rate of incarceration—a rate six to ten times the rate of other industrialized countries. This rate of incarceration costs the nation about $40 billion a year. And it disproportionately affects poor and minority populations. One in three young African American men is now under supervision of the criminal justice system—in prison or jail, or on probation or parole. A black male born today has a 29 percent chance of spending time in prison in his lifetime. (For more on how the United States deals with street criminals, check out the recently released Race to Incarcerate by Mark Mauer and The Sentencing Project (The New Press, 1999)).

When we released the Top 100 Corporate Criminals of the 1990s, we received a message from Robert Waldrop, the director of the Archbishop Oscar Romero Catholic Worker House in Oklahoma City.

Waldrop's Catholic Worker House feeds the poor, takes in people who are being evicted and generally helps those in need.

Having worked with the poor, Waldrop has come to the conclusion that in this country "you get all of the justice that you can afford to pay for." That's why the prisons aren't overrun with the executives and shareholders of our major corporate felons.

Waldrop has concluded that we should begin treating corporate criminals the way we treat street criminals.

So, he drew up a list of "Necessary Measures for Curbing the Corporate Crime Wave." Waldrop wrote the list "tongue in cheek," but he has gotten such a rave response to it that he believes that it might be the basis for a political movement to curb corporate crime.

After all, why should a corporate felon, its owners and managers, be allowed to influence our elections when an individual is stripped of his or her right to vote? It is time to start thinking about how to level the playing field.

With Waldrop's permission, we hereby reprint his "Eleven Necessary Measures for Curbing the Corporate Crime Wave."

1. The stockholders and management of corporations convicted of felonies should lose their right to vote and run for public office.

2. A registry should be maintained in each area of criminal corporations, and any corporation convicted of a felony should be required to register with the local police. A notice should be sent to all of their neighbors that a criminal corporation is taking up residence in their locality.

3. Criminal corporations should lose all corporate welfare benefits and government contracts.

4. Criminal corporations should be required to make weekly visits to parole officers, and their stockholders and management should be subject to random drug tests (either urine or hair).

5. Criminal corporations should not be allowed to operate within 500 yards of a school, church or library.

6. Criminal corporations should be required to place the phrase "A criminal corporation" on all advertising, signs and vehicles as a public warning.

7. If criminal corporations violate the terms of their parole, their stockholders and officers should go to jail.

8. In addition to the fine on the corporation, the personal assets of stockholders should be forfeited for their criminal negligence and lack of oversight.

9. The increasing number of lawless corporations calls for stricter penalties. Bring back the death penalty for corporations. In this context, the 'death penalty' is the closure of the corporation, the forfeiture of its assets to its victims and/or the government and the winding up of its affairs by a court appointed receiver.

10. Stockholders and management should be required to wear monitoring bracelets for the duration of their parole, and may not travel outside of their jurisdiction without a written pass from their parole officer.

11. The stockholders and management of criminal corporations may not associate with the stockholders and management of other corporate felons, and are forbidden to keep and bear arms.

Waldrop believes says that "the original conception of the corporation was limited—there had to be a definite public service."

"Now that whole concept has been stretched and there is no accountability," Waldrop says. He encourages readers to spread his list far and wide. And check out his other good works at his web site: http://www.justpeace.org.

The Corporate Century

December 29, 1999

As we move to the end of the millennium, it is important to remind ourselves that this has been the century of the corporation, where for-profit, largely unaccountable organizations with unlimited life, size and power took control of the economy and of the political economy—largely to the detriment of the individual consumer, worker, neighbor and citizen.

Let us again remind ourselves that corporations were the creation of the citizenry. (Thanks here to Richard Grossman of the Project on Corporations Law and Democracy for resurrecting and teaching us a history we would have collectively forgotten.)

In the beginning, we the citizenry created the corporation to do the public's work—build a canal or a road—and then go out of business. We asked people with money to build the canal or road. If anything went wrong, the liability of these people with money—shareholders, we call them—would be limited to the amount of money they invested and no more. This limited liability corporation is the bedrock of the market economy. The markets would deflate like a punctured balloon if corporations were stripped of limited liability for shareholders. And what do we, the citizenry, get in return for this generous public grant of limited liability? Originally, we told the corporation what to do. You are to deliver the goods and then go out of business. And then let humans live our lives. But corporations gained power, broke through democratic controls, and now roam around the world inflicting unspeakable damage on the earth. Let us count the ways: price-fixing, chemical explosions, mercury poisoning, oil spills, destruction of public transportation systems. Need concrete examples? These are five of the most egregious of the century:

Number five:
Archer Daniels Midland (ADM) and Price Fixing.

In October 1996, Archer Daniels Midland (ADM), the good people who bring you National Public Radio, pled guilty and paid a $100 million criminal fine—at the time, the largest criminal antitrust fine ever—for its role in conspiracies to fix prices to eliminate competition and allocate sales in the lysine and citric acid markets worldwide.

Number four:
Union Carbide and Bhopal.

In 1984, a Union Carbide pesticide factory in Bhopal, India released 90,000 pounds of the chemical methyl isocyanate. The resulting toxic cloud killed several thousand people and injured hundreds of thousands.

Number Three:
Chisso Corporation and Minamata.

Minamata, Japan was home to Chisso Corporation, a petrochemical company and maker of plastics. In the 1950s, fish began floating dead in Minamata Bay, cats began committing suicide, and children were getting rare forms of brain cancer. Thousands were injured. The company had been dumping mercury into the bay.

Number two:
Exxon Corporation and Valdez Oil Spill

Ten years ago, the Exxon Valdez hit a reef in Prince William Sound Alaska and spilled 11 million gallons of crude oil onto 1,500 miles of Alaskan shoreline, killing birds and fish, and destroying the way of life of thousands of Native Americans.

Number one:
General Motors and the Destruction of Inner City Rail.

Seventy years ago, clean, quiet and efficient inner city rail systems dotted the U.S. landscape. They were eliminated in the 1930s to make way for dirty and noisy gasoline-powered automobiles and buses. The inner city rail systems were destroyed by those very companies that would most benefit from destruction of inner city rail—oil, tire and automobile companies, led by General Motors. By 1949, GM had helped destroy 100 electric systems in New York, Philadelphia, Baltimore, St. Louis, Oakland, Salt Lake City, Los Angeles and elsewhere.

In 1949, a federal grand jury in Chicago indicted and a jury convicted GM, Standard Oil of California and Firestone, among others, of criminally conspiring to replace electric transportation with gas- and diesel-powered buses and to monopolize the sale of buses and related products to transportation companies around the country. GM and the other convicted companies were fined $5,000 each. These are not unusual examples. Books have been written documenting the ongoing destruction. The question remains—how do we put a stop to it? And the answer seems clear to us—reassert public control over what was originally a public institution. The ideas on how to reassert such control are the subject of debate and conflict, in Seattle and around the world. But it seems clear to us that as the twentieth century was the century of the corporation, the twenty-first promises to be the century where flesh-and-blood human beings reassert sovereignty over their lives, their markets and their democracy. Let us not forget that corporate control was never inevitable. They took it from us, and it is our responsibility to take it back.

Sixteen Years for a Snickers Bar

April 11, 2000

Last week, a Texas jury recommended that Kenneth Payne, 29, spend 16 years in jail.

Payne's crime? Stealing a Snickers bar from a Tyler, Texas grocery store on December 17, 1999.

When Smith County Assistant District Attorney Jodi Brown was asked by the Associated Press how she could justify 16 years for the theft of a Snickers bar, Brown replied "It was a king size."

A king size Snickers bar it was. Retail price: $1.

In Texas, if you steal property worth less than $500, it's a misdemeanor punishable by a fine of $500 with no jail time. The case was brought as a felony because Payne was a habitual offender. He had ten previous convictions—including one for stealing a bag of Oreo cookies—and had spent seven years in Texas prisons. When he shoved the king sized Snickers bar down his pants he was on parole for felony theft.

Still, the guy was a petty thief—he stole cookies and candy bars. Compare Kenneth Payne's plight to those of a group of white-collar and corporate criminals who also were sentenced this month.

Hoffman-LaRoche Ltd. pled guilty for their roles in an international conspiracy to suppress and eliminate competition in the vitamin industry—what the Justice Department calls perhaps the largest criminal antitrust conspiracy in history. The prison terms: four months, three and one-half months, three months and three months. (The four executives were also fined anywhere from $75,000 to $350,000).

Also this month, three cruise line employees were sentenced for their role in dumping pollution into the Alaskan Inland Passage from a Holland America cruise ship. The three employees were each sentenced to two years unsupervised probation and fined $10,000.

These are not unusual sentences for white-collar criminals. In fact, it is unusual to see a white-collar criminal do time.

So, how can it be that Kenneth Payne is doing 16 years for stealing a one dollar Snickers bar while the former executives of some of the world's largest corporations get off with a few months in prison—after being convicted of a crime that cost consumers hundreds of millions of dollars?

It's like Richard Pryor said—in our country—justice means "just us"—regular folks—and not them—the people who call the shots—who end up in the slammer.

This double standard permeates every aspect of our criminal justice system. The other day, for example, we were listening to National Public Radio, and up popped a debate about whether felons should be allowed to participate in a democracy.

On one side of the debate was Mark Mauer of the Sentencing Project. Mauer pointed out that in 46 states, you can't vote if you are in prison. In 16 states, if you were convicted of a felony—even if you get out of prison—you are disenfranchised for life. Mauer estimated that 13 percent of adult black men cannot vote as a result of a felony conviction right now. On the NPR show, Roger Clegg, an attorney with the right-leaning and the slightly misnamed Center for Equal Opportunity (Linda Chavez' think tank), made the argument that felons shouldn't be allowed to vote. "If you aren't willing to play by the rules, then you shouldn't have a say in making the rules," Clegg said.

"And people who have been convicted of felonies, which are by definition serious crimes, shouldn't be given a role in deciding how the government should be run," Clegg said.

After hearing this, we called up Clegg to ask what he thought about banning corporate criminals—like BASF and Hoffman LaRoche, who had engaged in perhaps the most egregious criminal antitrust conspiracy in history—from "deciding how the government should be run." (Corporations of course don't vote, but they do give money to elect candidates, they lobby legislators and law enforcement officials, and they mold public opinion through their public relations efforts.)

Gone was Clegg's unwavering absolutism.

After much humming and hawing, Clegg admitted that "it makes sense to limit the political role of corporations when they have shown that they are not worthy of trust." But he quickly added that "because individuals and corporations are fundamentally different, you can't just apply the rules equally." Clegg questioned whether the First Amendment would allow prosecutors to strip corporations of their "rights" to influence how the government should be run. Clegg, of course, raised no such question when it came to stripping individual felons of such "rights."

What about the death penalty? In a new book, *Actual Innocence: Five Days to Execution and Other Dispatches from the Wrongly Convicted* (Doubleday, 2000), Jim Dwyer, Peter Neufeld, Barry Scheck, report that in the 24 years since the death penalty was reinstated by the Supreme Court, about 620 individuals have been put to death—but 87 condemned persons had their convictions vacated by exonerating evidence.

Most likely, innocent lives have been taken. All this while really big recidivist corporate criminals like Exxon, Royal Caribbean, Rockwell International, Warner Lambert, Teledyne, and United Technologies—criminals truly deserving of the corporate death penalty, get away with slap on the wrist fines.

Bottom line: big corporations and white-collar criminals are getting away with it, while the political and media elites pull the wool over our eyes. Think of that next time you pick up a Snickers bar.

It's No Accident

November 2, 2000

Imagine this: You are a prosecutor. You indict a person for homicide. You type up a press release and plan to hold a press conference to announce the indictment.

But before you say anything to the media about the indictment, you must first consult with the lawyer for the defendant. And under the law, the lawyer for the defendant has a right to veto anything you say in the press release, or at the press conference. And the lawyer for the defendant has the right to negotiate the wording of the press release.

No prosecutor in his or her right mind would accept such an intrusion by a person accused of a crime.

But a similar situation is being tolerated by the Consumer Product Safety Commission (CPSC), the federal policing agency set up to enforce consumer protection laws, including those covering children's products made by companies such as Hasbro (Playskool), Mattel (Fisher-Price), Graco/Century Products, Evenflo, Cosco, Safety 1st and Kolcraft.

Under the law that set up the CPSC, before the agency releases information to the public, it must notify the company of its intention. If the company disputes the accuracy or fairness of the information to be released, then the general counsel of the CPSC gets involved and the dispute over the press release could end up in federal court. But the CPSC is strapped for resources, and the result is, in most cases, the company gets its way.

What's the consequence of such a policy? More than most, this policing agency has become subordinate to the industry it polices. And the result is that hundreds of innocent children are killed and thousands are injured by consumer products every year—products that would have been pulled off the market by an independent agency not hamstrung by corporate interference.

One such infant who died was Danny Keysar. In May 1998, 17-month old Danny was at a daycare home. His daycare provider put him down for a nap in a Playskool Travel-Lite portable crib. A short while later, when she went to check on him, she found that the crib had collapsed with Danny in it. His neck was caught in the rails. He wasn't breathing. He died.

Marla Felcher, then a professor of marketing at Northwestern University, was a friend of Danny's parents. She attended Danny's funeral. At the funeral, Danny's mother urged Felcher to investigate why Danny died.

Within a week of beginning her investigation, Felcher realized that Danny's death should never have happened. The crib that killed Danny had been recalled five years earlier. Danny was the fifth child to be killed by this particular Playskool portable crib model. Other companies manufactured cribs using the same design. And over 1.5 million units of other portable cribs had been recalled, and at least a dozen children have been killed in total.

The whole idea of the portable crib is that it collapses easily. The top rails on these types of portable cribs have a hinge in the center. A child could stand up, grab onto the top rail, and collapse it. Danny's weight was strong enough to collapse the crib. When cribs of this sort collapse, the top rail bends at the center hinge, forms a "V" and the child is knocked down. His neck or chest can get caught in the grip of the V, and he is no longer able to breathe.

The problem with the Playskool crib and others that were designed the same way is that it is possible for a caregiver to set up the crib and assume that it is locked into place, when it is not.

"The coroners' reports on all these portable crib fatalities are shockingly similar—the kid was found trapped in the 'V' of the folded crib rails," Felcher told us last week.

The control that the consumer product industry has over the CPSC is truly mindboggling. For example, some products pose a serious risk of injury to children, while others present only a slight risk. But because the industry has a stranglehold over the information flow from CPSC to the public, reporters and consumer never find out whether the risk is serious or not.

Thus while the CPSC rates how dangerous a product is— A, B, C, D—the rating is not made public. And because the CPSC is not aggressive in getting information out about product hazards, when it does recall a dangerous product, a very small percentage—perhaps 10 to 30 percent—of the product gets pulled off the market. One of those recalled products that failed to get pulled from the market was the crib that killed Danny Keysar.

Felcher has written up the findings of her investigation in a book (*It's No Accident: How the Infant Products Industry Compromises Baby Safety* (Common Courage Press, February 2001)). And Danny's parents have set up a non-profit to help get dangerous children's products off the market (www.kidsin-danger.org).

But true progress won't be made until a new political culture sweeps Washington, one that values human life over the almighty dollar. Only then will the police be liberated from the death grip of the corporate elite.

Ball Park Franks Fiasco: 21 Dead, $200,000 Fine

July 25, 2001

Let us now have a moment of silence for the victims of the Ball Park Franks fiasco.

Thank you.

This is the situation: Bil Mar Foods is a unit of the Chicago-based giant Sara Lee Corporation, the maker of pound cakes, cheesecakes, pies, muffins, L'Eggs, Hanes, Playtex and Wonderbra products—your typical food and underwear conglomerate.

Bil Mar makes hot dogs—Ball Park franks hot dogs. You've seen them when you go to a baseball game at Tiger Stadium in Detroit and elsewhere.

Last month, Sara Lee pled guilty to two misdemeanor counts in connection with a listeriosis outbreak that led to the deaths of at least 21 consumers who ate Ball Park Franks hot dogs and other meat products. One hundred people were seriously injured. The company paid a $200,000 fine.

According to Kenneth Moll, a Chicago attorney representing the families of the victims, this is what happened:

Bil Mar has a hot dog facility in Zeeland, Michigan. The company shut down the facility over the July 4th weekend of 1998 to replace a refrigeration unit that was above the hot processing facility. The hot dogs are heated at one end and sent down a conveyer belt to the other.

Moll's theory is that the removal of the air conditioning unit and its replacement dislodged some dangerous bacteria in the ceiling. When the plant reopened, steam from the passing hot dogs went up to the ceiling, condensed and dripped back down with the dangerous bacteria onto the hot dogs.

In November 1998, Paul Mead from the Centers for Disease Control (CDC) in Atlanta started receiving calls from the state health departments around the country that had isolated strains of a deadly bacteria, Listeria monocytogenes.

Mead looked at the bacteria and found that they were the same strain. He sent out questionnaires and discovered there was an open package of hot dogs in the home of one of the people who died. The CDC tested the hot dogs and isolated the same bacterial strain—a DNA fingerprint of the type of bacteria.

According to Moll, Mead went to the Bil Mar plant in Zeeland, Michigan and tested unopened packages of hot dogs and was able to isolate the same DNA fingerprint bacteria. In December 1998, Sara Lee ordered a recall of millions of pounds of hot dogs and deli meats.

According to a series of reports in the *Detroit Free Press*, plant workers were regularly testing work surfaces for the presence of cold-loving bacteria—a class of bacteria that includes the deadly Listeria monocytogenes as well as some harmless bacteria.

According to the *Free Press*, beginning in July 1998, after the replacement of the old refrigeration unit, workers recorded a sharp increase in the presence of cold-loving bacteria. The number of positive samples remained high until the company stopped performing tests in November 1998—a month before the Sara Lee recall.

"Sara Lee was doing testing of the environment in the plant for cold-loving bacteria," said Caroline Smith DeWaal of the Center for Science in the Public Interest. "Then their tests started coming up positive, so they stopped testing. They knew they had a problem with bacteria in the plant. But instead of solving it, they chose to ignore it."

This is crucial, because if the company knew that they were had a Listeria monocytogenes problem and ignored it, they could be hit with a felony conviction. And felony convictions have all kinds of collateral consequences, including possible loss of federal contracts—Sara Lee had a big hot dog contract with the Department of Defense.

In an interview, U.S. Attorney Phillip Green said there

was insufficient evidence to bring a felony charge.

"There was simply no evidence that Sara Lee Bil Mar knew that the food product that they were producing and shipping out was adulterated with Listeria monocytogenes," Green told us.

When asked about the allegations raised by the Free Press that the company was testing for cold-loving bacteria, Green told us, "the testing that you are referring to is known as Low Temperature Pathogens testing—that is a very general test that does not necessarily indicate the presence of Listeria monocytogenes."

"The USDA regulations don't require a plant to conduct testing on finished product for the presence of deadly pathogens such as Listeria monocytogenes," Green said. "And Bil Mar was following accepted industry practices in conducting general testing for the low temperature pathogens."

But Green refused to answer specific questions about evidence concerning a possible felony violation.

Moll—the attorney representing the victims—told us that the evidence "does necessarily indicate the presence of Listeria monocytogenes." The CDC's Mead found studies showing that, had Sara Lee done further testing for the deadly strain of listeria, almost half of the cold-loving bacteria could have tested positive for Listeria monocytogenes.

But U.S. Attorney Green never read Mead's report. He never called on Mead, perhaps the crucial expert in this case, to testify before the grand jury.

In fact, it is apparent from our investigation into this matter that federal prosecutors were overpowered by Sara Lee's outside lawyers in this case—the Chicago firm of Jenner & Block, led by former Chicago U.S. Attorney Anton Valukas.

Valukas refused, on advice of his client, to speak with us.

But the extraordinary degree of the collaboration between Sara Lee and the federal prosecutors in this case can be seen on Sara Lee's web site where it has posted a "joint press release."

No, that's not a typo. The U.S. Attorney and Sara Lee

issued a joint press release announcing the plea agreement in which no mention is made of Ball Park Franks hot dogs.

The issuance of a joint press release is an extraordinary event. U.S. Attorney Green can't name a case where the prosecutor and convict issued a joint press release announcing their plea agreement. Neither can the current chief of the Criminal Division at the Department of Justice, Michael Chertoff. He calls it "unusual."

In a number of ways, the Sara Lee prosecution brings home the double standards in our criminal justice system.

A company pleads guilty to a crime that leads to the death of 21 human beings. The company pleads to two misdemeanors. The company is fined $200,000. Think about that.

We were so outraged by this that we went over to the White House and asked President Bush's press secretary about it.

We laid out the facts of the Sara Lee case and then asked our question. This is how it went:

Question: Ari, has the President expressed a view on the death penalty for corporate criminals—that is, revoking the charter of a corporation that has been convicted of a crime that has resulted in death?

Fleischer: The President does not weigh in on those matters of justice. They should not be dictated by decisions made at the White House.

Question: Now, Ari, wait a second. Ari, Ari, wait a second. He's in favor of the death penalty for individuals generally. Is he in favor of the death penalty for corporations convicted of crimes that result in death?

Fleischer: These are questions that are handled by officials of the Justice Department—not by people at the White House.

Someday, Ari, the White House too will have to answer— why death to individual criminals, but not to your corporate criminal paymasters?

When In Doubt, Shred It

January 11, 2002

Arthur Andersen, one of the nation's Big Five accounting firms, admitted this week that it destroyed a "significant" number of documents related to its audit of Enron, the Houston, Texas-based energy trading giant that collapsed spectacularly into a pile of worthless securities late last year, wiping out $30 billion worth of shareholder value—but not before top executives bailed out early.

The Enron practice of shifting liabilities off the books to more than 3,500 subsidiaries raised so many red flags that you'd think you were in a military parade somewhere in China.

As the criminal investigation geared up this week, Attorney General John Ashcroft and the entire staff of the U.S. Attorney's office in Houston recused itself from the investigation. The whole bunch has been conflicted out. The investigation is going to be headed by Michael Chertoff, head of the Justice Department's criminal division.

Whether justice can be had in a case where both Enron and the accounting industry has marinated Washington in campaign cash is unclear.

What is clear is that Enron and the accounting industry were so drunk with their corporate power that they mistook a modest proposed rule that might have prevented the Enron collapse for a threat to their profits and nuked it.

In the summer of 2000, Securities and Exchange Commission Chair Arthur Levitt sought to pass a rule that would have said to accounting firms—if you are going to audit a client, you can't take consulting fees from that client.

The accounting industry went bananas. Why? Because they see audits as a way to get a foot in the door of big companies. First audit the company, then ream the company for exorbitant management fees.

But Levitt insisted that auditors be "independent" of the

clients they audit. How can an auditor be independent if at the same time it's auditing the company, it's raking in millions in consulting fees?

With Levitt's proposed rule, the accounting industry saw a booming profit center threatened, and it began to marshal its friends—both Democratic and Republican alike—in Washington to beat back the Levitt rule. And beat it back they did. Congressional leaders told Levitt, in no uncertain terms, that if he proceeded, they would slash the SEC's budget. Levitt backed down.

Last year, while Andersen was paid $27 million for its audit work at Enron, it received $28 million in management consulting fees from the same Enron.

Let's say that Andersen's audit partner in Houston saw the red flags, and began to raise questions. Are Andersen executives going to risk losing the lucrative consulting contract by offending the company with a harsh audit? Probably not.

As for the destruction of documents, let's put it this way— much of the history of corporate crime and violence in this country has never seen the light of day because of corporate

executives who follow closely the advise of corporate counsel—
when in doubt, shred it.

Corporate lawyers have become so cavalier about the subject that they publicly discuss destruction of documents.

Andersen was apparently following to the letter advice
often dished out by white collar defense lawyers, including that
of Harvey Pitt, the accounting industry star defense lawyer until
he became chair of the Securities and Exchange Commission.
(Pitt will probably have to recuse himself from the Andersen
investigation because he did work for the firm when in private
practice.)

White collar defense lawyers like Pitt often advise corporate clients to implement flexible "document retention" programs so that incriminating documents are destroyed before
they see the light of day.

In 1994, Pitt co-authored a law review article ("When Bad
Things Happen to Good Companies: A Crisis Management
Primer").

"At the crux of many corporate crises, there are typically a
handful of key documents," Pitt wrote. "Corporate counsel must
take every available opportunity to imbue company executives
with the understanding that their documents will take on separate lives when they enter the treadmill of litigation. ... Ask
executives and employees to imagine all their documents in the
hands of a zealous regulator or on the front page of the New
York Times. ... Each company should have a system of determining the retention and destruction of documents," Pitt wrote.
"Obviously, once a subpoena has been issued, or is about to be
issued, any existing document destruction policies should be
brought to an immediate halt."

Former Securities and Exchange Commission enforcement chief John Fedders, writing in a 1980 law review article
titled "Document Retention and Destruction: Practical, Legal
and Ethical Considerations," took this advice one step further.

"On occasion, counsel will be shown a document which

could expose the corporation to liability if it became available to adverse parties," Fedders wrote. "If the document is not yet scheduled for destruction under the terms of the program, management may advocate a waiver of the program to allow the document to be promptly destroyed."

Things are destined to get worse before they get better. The SEC has the accounting industry's pit bull as its chair. In addition, Bush has nominated two new SEC commissioners, both of whom are former partners of big five accounting firms— Paul Atkins, a partner with PricewaterhouseCoopers, and Cynthia Glassman of Ernst & Young.

That gives the accounting industry absolute control over what was once the top cop on the corporate crime beat. Get ready for more Enrons.

Cracking Down on Corporate Crime, Really

July 3, 2002

Here is one of the most remarkable aspects of the still-unfolding financial scandals swirling around Worldcom, Xerox, Global Crossing, Enron, Arthur Andersen, Tyco and a growing number of other companies: The fraud occurred in the most heavily regulated and monitored area of corporate activity.

If an epidemic of corporate malfeasance could occur in the financial arena, how serious is the more general problem of corporate crime?

Consider the checks and balances in place that should have stemmed the wave of corporate wrongdoing which has reportedly angered even American CEO George Bush:

- Disclosure requirements for corporate financial performance are extensive, and by far the most detailed for any element of corporate activity.
- There is a distinct industry—made up of accounting firms—whose function is to review the financial numbers, audit corporate books and certify the validity of financial statements.
- There is another distinct industry, separate from the accountants—this is the Wall Street investment firms—whose function is to scrutinize the corporate reports, interview corporate executives, analyze market performance and provide investors with independent evaluations of company prospects.
- There is a legal duty for corporate executives to advance the interest of an important and powerful class of people—shareholders—and significant numbers of these shareholders are increasingly organized and assertive of their rights (including through pension funds). There is no comparable legal duty for corporate executives to serve consumer or worker interests, say.
- An array of Securities and Exchange Commission regula-

tions establish rules for financial reporting, and are backed by the enforcement power of the agency, as well as the threat of private litigation from shareholders in case of violation.

Other aspects of corporate activity are simply not subject to such robust scrutiny and control.

Given what is now the apparent blatant corporate disregard for the law, even in areas where executives are most closely watched, what should we expect is occurring elsewhere? What's happening with consumer rip-offs, sales of unsafe products, endangerment of workers, pollution of the environment?

Even with inadequate law enforcement, reporting requirements or organized countervailing institutions, we know enough to know that the epidemic of corporate crime, fraud and abuse is at least as severe outside of the financial arena as within.

To take just two examples from recent months: In May, drug maker Schering-Plough signed a consent decree with the Food and Drug Administration, agreeing to pay a record $500 million in connection with charges that over a three-year period it produced about 125 different prescription and over-the-counter drugs in factories that failed to comply with good manufacturing practice. And in April, the Justice Department announced that it collected more than $1.3 billion in 2001 in connection with enforcement actions related to health care fraud, and that last year 465 defendants were convicted for health-care fraud crimes. This kind of revelation occurs regularly, but news accounts rarely combine them—as they are now doing with the financial scandals—to make clear the breadth and depth of the problem.

With the most recent round of disclosures of financial wrongdoing at Worldcom and other companies, it no longer appears that Big Business's Congressional allies are going to be able to block all meaningful remedial measures, and the Bush administration is now preparing a reform package.

If those reforms are limited to addressing financial fraud, however, the biggest and most serious corporate criminal activity will be able to flourish.

What we need is a full set of restraints on corporate crime. But even small steps could significantly reduce the toll of corporate crime and violence. Here are three measures that should be adopted this year, before Congress recesses and momentum for corporate reform slows:

First, the Federal Bureau of Investigation should be required to compile an annual report on corporate crime in American, to accompany its current Crime in the United States report, which is unfortunately confined to street crime.

Second, the federal government should refuse to do business with companies that are serious and/or repeat lawbreakers, as well as deny other privileges (for example, granting broadcasting licenses) to corporate criminals. This would involve some new or strengthened laws and regulations, as well more stringent enforcement of debarment, contractor responsibility and good character laws now on the books. States and local governments should adopt similar measures.

Third, whistleblowers and private citizens should be able to enforce laws regulating corporate conduct. One way to facilitate this enforcement approach would be to expand and creatively adapt the False Claims Act, which currently enables whistleblowers to initiate lawsuits against entities which have defrauded the government, and which reclaims for the government every year hundreds of millions of dollars stolen by unethical contractors.

"Cracking down on corporate crime"—the mantra of the moment—cannot be limited just to financial crime, already the most policed form of corporate wrongdoing.

PART TWO

BELTWAY BANDITS AND WELFARE CHEATS

Political corruption has been institutionalized in the United States.

While out-and-out bribery and vote-buying certainly persists, much more important is the massive infusion of corporate money into the political process and the revolving door between government and business.

The money enters via political action committee contributions to candidates for Congress, unlimited "soft money" donations to political parties, an orgy of fundraising events at the political parties' national conventions, and "independent" expenditures by corporations and trade associations in political campaigns.

There are very personal interests at stake, as well. Many Members of Congress and their staffs, cabinet officers and regulatory agency leaders expect to leave public service for careers in Parasitic Washington: the lobby shops, trade associations, high-powered law firms, government affairs offices and public relations firms that seek to gain influence in the corridors of power. Part of the deal is that, while they are in office, they pay attention to those who have already made the shift from government to the private sector.

The complement to political corruption is business's extraordinary power to threaten to move production to a different jurisdiction. Especially at the state level, what corporations cannot exact by way of bribes, they often win with threats, overt or implied, to move operations

Political corruption and business coercion yield concrete results: an endless array of goodies for the corporations who invest in politics—special tax breaks, government giveaways, regulatory nods and winks, even an occasional trade action against close allies.

In recent years, political cynicism and opportunism have reached new lows. With the tragedy of 9-11 and ongoing fears of terrorism used as rationalizations to ram through Congress and administrative agencies a variety of corporate goodies, many with no plausible connection to national security

For the last 25 years, without interruption, corporations have had strong allies in the White House. We've gone to the Bush II White House regularly to ask about one or another manifestation of the corporate grip on policymaking in the most business-friendly administration of the last 100 years. Besides the standard evasion and deception, the common response to our queries is belittlement. The undercurrent of the non-answers to such queries—Don't you understand how Washington works?

Marriott:
Corporate Schoolyard Bully

March 12, 1999

Call Marriott the latest in a long line of corporate school-yard bullies. The hotel chain in March exacted an enormous tax and road improvement subsidy from the state of Maryland and Maryland's Montgomery County, in exchange for a promise to do nothing.

Actually, the company promised to proceed with existing plans to hire 700 new workers at the headquarters and not to move its headquarters out of Montgomery County (just north of Washington, D.C.) and across the border into Virginia.

If the company chooses to expand its current headquarters, the value of the Maryland package will be $31.68 million over 19 years. If the company builds a new headquarters, the value of the Maryland gift will rise to up to $44.17 million.

Maryland offered Marriott the giveaway for one reason: it feared the company would jump to low-tax haven Virginia—an impression stoked both by Virginia and the hotel company. Current Governor James Gilmore III and former Virginia Governor George Allen both tried to seduce company chair Bill Marriott to border hop.

Faced with Virginia's enticements, and with Marriott playing coy about its final decision, Maryland progressively elevated its offer to the hotel company.

When Marriott announced that it would stay in Maryland, state officials celebrated their victory over their neighbor. "Our team is red hot, Virginia's team is all shot," Maryland House Speaker Casper Taylor, a Democrat, told the *Washington Post*.

But in the bidding war that Marriott forced between Maryland and Virginia, there was only one true winner: Marriott.

The state and county subsidies that Marriott extracted from Maryland constitute one of the worst and most indefensible kinds of corporate welfare.

Because such a high percentage of state and local property taxes are allocated to schools, tax abatements of the sort showered on Marriott frequently come at the expense of school funding. Some states wall off school funding from tax abatements—meaning the burden is instead shifted directly to other taxpayers to make up the lost income.

And there is not even the pretense that Maryland-style giveaways create or preserve jobs. Based on company growth, profitability and needs, for example, Marriott had determined to expand its headquarters, irrespective of whether it would receive tax breaks from the headquarter's home state.

Not even proponents of the giveaway deal can rationalize the subsidy on the grounds that it created jobs that would not otherwise have been created—the best they can argue is that they are in Maryland, rather than somewhere else. While Maryland officials can therefore attempt to justify the tax abatements on the grounds that they preserved Maryland jobs, from a broader social point of view it is clear this kind of giveaway is a direct transfer from taxpayers or schools to the company with no reciprocal benefits.

Unfortunately, Marriott's corporate blackmail of Maryland is now the norm in corporate location decisions. These threats are "rampant" and "business as usual," says Greg LeRoy of Good Jobs First, a Washington, D.C. advocacy group working to promote accountability among corporations receiving job subsidies.

In many cities and states, virtually no major building is built, no large corporate headquarters lease renewed, no Fortune 500 factory opened, without a slew of tax breaks and related subsidies. The most outrageous example, says LeRoy, is the New York City gift to the New York Stock Exchange—a subsidy of $600 million to $900 million to keep the Exchange from migrating to New Jersey. And each giveaway sets the stage for additional subsidy demands from other large employers.

Similar largesse is rarely bestowed on small business own-ers, raising the question of why the Big Boys can't pay their fair share, as the little guys do.

Frequently, company threats to move are a bluff. Decisions on where to locate major facilities are generally made based on transportation costs, company history, access to suppliers and other factors that override state and local tax costs. But often enough the threats are real, especially if the choice is between nearby locations.

And it is very difficult for cities and states to know when companies' threats are empty. "It is easy to create a credible appearance" of an intent to move, says LeRoy, and plenty of consultants are ready to present analyses to the public on how a company can save money by locating elsewhere.

The plausibility of the threat notwithstanding, local and state officials that have the backbone to stand up to corporate bullies can often win. If they are going to back down and offer subsidies, LeRoy advises at least demanding contractual guaran-tees that promised jobs will be created and retained.

An ultimate solution to the problem of corporate mobili-ty will require aggressive national action. Representative David Minge, D-Minnesota, has proposed a federal excise tax on com-panies receiving state and local tax breaks—a good first step to take back some of the lunch money that the corporate school-yard bullies steal from intimidated states, counties and towns.

Al Gore, Corporate Welfare Environmentalist

March 7, 2000

Gas prices are rising and the threat of global warming looms ever larger. Al Gore, what have you done to wean the United States from its oil dependency?

Asked a related question in a recent debate with Bill Bradley ("We sent our armed forces to the Persian Gulf in 1991 to return a country to its owners. Now we see higher gas prices. What will you do to ensure this does not happen again?"), Gore responded:

"We have an interest in being less dependent on sources of oil from a region that is, over time, vulnerable to instability. I helped to put in place a program called the Partnership for a New Generation of Vehicles, which commits the big three automakers in our country to getting new vehicles into the marketplace that have three times the efficiency of today's vehicles."

It was telling that Al "Earth in the Balance" Gore would point to the relatively obscure Partnership for a New Generation of Vehicles (PNGV), the epitome of what might be called corporate welfare environmentalism.

The Partnership for a New Generation of Vehicles (PNGV) is a public-private partnership between seven federal agencies, 20 federal laboratories, and the big three automakers—General Motors, Ford and what is now Daimler Chrysler.

PNGV's main long term goal is to develop a "Supercar," "an environmentally friendly car with up to triple the fuel efficiency of today's midsize cars—without sacrificing affordability, performance or safety."

It is hard to imagine an industry less in need of government support for research than the highly capitalized auto industry. Ford pulled in profits of $5.4 billion in the first three quarters of 1999. GM earned $4.8 billion over the same period.

The government is supporting research that the industry could easily do on its own (and, to some extent, is doing apart from the PNGC initiative), and should be mandated to undertake to meet tougher environmental standards.

How is it that the competitors in the oligopolistic auto industry are able to undertake a joint research undertaking? The PNGV program gives participants an effective exemption from antitrust laws.

Defenders of such collaborative efforts love to invoke the legendary example of the Manhattan Project, but the evidence is overwhelming that innovation—especially in the commercial sector—is more likely to result from competition in research and development.

Oligopolistic collaboration is prone to all kinds of pitfalls, from bureaucratic sloth to corrupt suppression of research—as the auto industry's own history makes clear.

In the 1960s, the Justice Department filed suit against the automakers for product fixing—for refusing to introduce air quality enhancing technologies. Among other claims, the Justice Department alleged that the U.S. automakers and their trade association had conspired "to eliminate all competition among themselves in the research, development, manufacture and installation of motor vehicle air pollution control equipment."

Now the Clinton-Gore administration has stamped its official imprimatur on the industry's preferred anti-competitive coordination of environmental research. (The administration's happy-talk calls it "pre-competitive.")

Maybe today's auto industry is different than the auto industry of the 1960s. Or, maybe not.

Above all, the PNGV initiative has served during the Clinton-Gore administration as a smokescreen behind which the automakers hide to protect themselves from more stringent air quality standards.

"Cynics think that the PNGV was simply a politically

astute 10-year reprieve for the domestic auto industry from threats of higher Corporate Average Fuel Efficiency standards," writes Earth Day founder Denis Hayes in his new book, *The Official Earth Day Guide to Planet Repair*.

Deployment of existing technologies could dramatically enhance auto fuel efficiency and reduce greenhouse gas emissions, but the automakers—who have waged a decades-long crusade against mandatory fuel efficiency standards—choose not to make these technologies widely available.

And the PNGV program does not even require the deployment in mass production of the technologies it seeks to develop.

The leading innovators in fuel efficiency have been Toyota and Honda, which do not participate in the PNGV program.

"By 2004, the PNGV hopes U.S. manufacturers will be able to produce a U.S. vehicle that has roughly the same characteristics as the already-on-the-market Toyota Prius," Hayes notes.

"Actually," Hayes writes, "the most likely 2004 PNGV vehicles will be inferior to the Prius in one important regard: they will probably use diesel instead of gasoline engines....Sadly and ironically, the cars produced by the decade-long, multiple-billion-dollar PNGV effort may be banned from California—the nation's largest automobile market—because they cause too much pollution."

No such criticism is voiced by the corporate welfare environmentalists in the Clinton-Gore administration. They are eagerly planning to launch 21st-Century Truck Initiative, a public-private partnership for truck manufacturers modeled on the PNGV.

Stop Corruption Now

May 30, 2000

Last Wednesday, we walked down to the MCI Center to catch the "National Tribute to President Clinton."

Out in front of the MCI Center, Doris Haddock, Granny D., the grandmom who walked across the country protesting money in politics, was being interviewed by reporters.

Granny D and about 12 of her supporters had just been sentenced to a $10 fine for protesting earlier this year under the Capitol Rotunda.

The sentencing judge said he felt guilty that he wasn't with the defendants protesting that day, and so he let them off easy.

Fresh off that sentencing victory, the troops, led by Granny D, stormed down to the MCI Center, where Clinton and the Democratic National Committee were in the process of raising $26.5 million in one night.

This event reeked of corruption, coming as it did at the end of a day when Congress made it easier for American corporations to put down their collective footprint on China—and in exchange, American corporations funneled big money into the two major parties. (The word went out that the vote had to be taken during the day so Members of Congress and the lobbyists could make it to the MCI Center and across town to a similar Republican fundraiser in time for dinner and the festivities that followed.)

Outside on F Street, we chanted and carried signs, but President Clinton, Vice President Al Gore, Hillary and Tipper, and Terry McAuliffe, of course, were out of sight and out of earshot. So, we needed to get in, and like beggars at a NCAA Final Four tournament game, we found ourselves walking up and down the sidewalk whispering "need two tickets." And we came across a union guy who had a stack, and handed us three.

So, three of us walked in to witness an amazing spectacle.

There on the ground floor, where people usually play basketball and hockey, were people eating dinner. To get to eat dinner down there, we learned, you would have to raise $50,000 to $500,000 for the Democratic Party.

Up above, in the rafters, were the regular folks—13,000 regular types who the Dems said paid $50 and $100 a piece. (In reality, the only way they got that many people in to watch Bill and Al and Lenny Kravitz and Robin Williams was to give away the tickets for free. Our ticket says "Price: 0.00" How many of those do you have to sell to raise $26.5 million?)

Anyway, a grotesque spectacle it was. And especially sickening was the performance of Terry McAuliffe, the fundraiser who pulled the whole thing off. He went on and on about how the Dems are different from the Republicans. We wear blue jeans, they wear tuxedos. We take the subway, they come in limos. We eat ribs, they eat steak. What a crock.

In fact, Terry, you both are marinated in Fortune 500 cash and you both stink for it. So, after Terry made his fake populist case that the Dems are with the people, and the Republicans are not, President Bill was introduced. Then, out of the darkness of the MCI Center, a group of dissenters began chanting—"Stop Corruption Now, Stop Corruption Now, Stop Corruption Now."

A visibly angry Bill, not wanting America to hear the dissenters, shouted to sidekick Terry—"Turn this (microphone) off, and turn this one on—if you turn this on, they can hear me instead of them."

Then the Great Corrupter defended himself against the dissenters' charge of corruption. "I don't believe it's corruption to take money to pass the Brady bill," he said. "To pass the Family and Medical Leave Bill, so people can take some time off when their family members are ill. To pass the Patient's Bill of Rights... I don't think that is corruption. That's good for America." And then he turned to Terry and smirked. As if to say—teach them wimps to holler during my speech.

Those, of course, are not examples of corruption, Bill.

It is, most recently, the China bill that reeks of corruption, with Big Business spending big money on both parties and both parties delivering at the other end, despite compelling arguments that granting Permanent Trade Status to China would injure workers and farmers in both countries, while further fattening the pockets of the people eating dinner on the floor of the MCI Center.

Which way out of this quagmire? One first step is to organize to open up this year's Presidential Debates to different voices. Al Gore and George Bush walk in unison on many issues dear to corporate America—as the China vote made clear. Third party candidates not beholden to corporate power must be heard.

George Bush and Al Gore fear such an open-ended debate. But the alternative is mass boredom, a further decline in the percentage of Americans who vote, and corrosive drip from a corrupt political machine that threatens the remnants of democratic government.

Bud Bowl III

October 16, 2000

Our families like it when we go off to cover a presidential debate. That's because when we come back from one, we bring back bags full of goodies.

After the second debate, we drove home from Winston-Salem with a C-Span canvas bag that included Matchbox racing cars (paid for by 3Com), Budweiser beer mugs (from Anheuser Busch) and a handful of ATT pre-paid long distance phone cards ("proud technology sponsor of the Presidential Debates").

From the Boston debate, we came back with t-shirts, baseball caps, a canvas bag, reporters notebooks, pens, key chains.

The food and beer at the debates are being provided by Anheuser-Busch. Post-debates, the Starbucks coffee and Krispy Kreme donuts are on the house. (Why would any reporter in his or her right mind choose to walk a half a mile through police lines, horse manure and pepper spray to cover hundreds of young people protesting Green Party candidate Ralph Nader's exclusion from the debates and forgo watching the Yankees in the playoffs while sipping a cold Budweiser?)

The Ford Motor Co. logo is emblazoned on the plastic press pass holder.

In Boston, before slipping the Ford press pass over over our heads, we held a moment of silence for the hundreds of innocents killed while riding unstable Ford sports utility vehicles on frayed Firestone tires.

We guessed Jim Lehrer wouldn't ask the corporate candidates on stage whether or not they favored a criminal homicide investigation of these two companies and the responsible executives for the deaths of these innocents. He didn't.

Remarkably, the hundreds of reporters covering these debates think little of the corporate sponsorship of the debates. (Or if they are thinking about it at all, few choose to express their thoughts in print.)

Thirteen years ago, the two major parties hijacked the presidential debates away from the League of Women Voters, after the League made the mistake of opening the debates to third party candidate John Anderson in 1980.

To replace the League, the two parties set up a front called Commission on Presidential Debates (it is run out of a political consulting firm's office off of Dupont Circle in Washington, D.C.) to set rules that would effectively exclude third party candidates.

Big companies—Anheuser-Busch, U.S. Airways and 3Com—put up big money to sponsor the debates. Anheuser Busch, for example, paid $500,000 to be the "exclusive" sponsor for the debate in St. Louis.

Not coincidentally, the only two candidates who seriously question the power of giant corporations over our political economy—Nader and Reform Party candidate Patrick Buchanan—have been banned from the conversation.

The Commission says that there are more than 100 candidates for president this year and you can't fit them all onto the stage, and that's why they set the bar at 15 percent in the polls. Candidates polling less than 15 percent are excluded from all three of the Commission debates.

But such a standard would have excluded Jesse Ventura, the former wrestler whose debate success catalyzed his victorious gubernatorial campaign, from the debates in Minnesota. A more reasonable standard would be five percent in the polls, which would cut the field to two, three or four. Or you could ask the public who they would like to see in the debates. (More than half want to see Buchanan and Nader in.)

But far be it for us to complain. We say—bring on Bud Bowl Three. Can't wait to see what we get in our canvas bags in St. Louis.

The Corporate Conservative Administration

January 11, 2001

Compassionate conservativism?

Try corporate conservativism. It's corporate conservatism that is going to be the defining feature of the Bush White House.

Pushing beyond the corporate corrupting frontiers blazed by the Clinton administration, the Bush team is making clear that it intends to deliver on its campaign promises to strengthen Big Business's grip over government policy-making.

The Bush cabinet is drawing on corporate executives as much or more than any previous administration. Andrew Card, set to be Bush's chief of staff, moves to the White House from a posting as General Motors vice president. Previous to that position, he ran the auto industry's lobby shop. Bush has tapped Paul O'Neill, chair of Alcoa, to head his Treasury Department. Bush crony Don Evans, the Commerce Secretary-designee, is CEO of Tom Brown, Inc., an oil company. Donald Rumsfeld, the Bush nominee to head the Pentagon, is former CEO of G.D. Searle and of General Instrument, and has held a variety of other top corporate posts. Bush's nominee for Veterans Affairs Secretary, Anthony Principi, is president of a wireless telecommunications company. National Security Adviser-designate Condoleeza Rice is a member of the board of directors of Chevron (which has christened an oil tanker, the Condoleeza Rice) and Charles Schwab, and is a member of J.P. Morgan's International Advisory Council.

Of course, both George W. Bush and Dick Cheney (CEO of Halliburton, the oil services firm) themselves both come from the oil industry.

Bush's transition team is dominated by high donors and corporate interests. Of the 474 individuals on the transition team, 261 made political contributions during the last election cycle, the Center for Responsive Politics reports—and 95 percent of the $5.3 million they contributed went to Republican candidates or the Republican Party.

Even more telling is the overwhelming corporate background of the transition team members.

The transition team for the Department of Energy, for example, is almost exclusively made up of people affiliated with or working for the extractive energy industry. Companies and outfits represented include: Phillips Petroleum, Enron, Kennecott, Southern California Edison, the National Mining Association and the Nuclear Energy Institute.

For the Department of Health and Human Services transition, the drug, biotech, insurance and hospital industries are set to have their way. The transition team includes representatives from Merck, the American Hospital Association, Mutual of Omaha, BIO (the biotech trade group), Ernst and Young and the National Association of Health Underwriters.

On the Department of Labor transition team, you find two members of the Teamsters, and no other labor-affiliated representatives. Instead, the transition team comes from Union Pacific, the National Restaurant Association, the American Trucking Association, the National Mining Association, the U.S. Chamber of Commerce and the Society of Human Resource Managers.

It's unlikely that the transition team members—at least as a body—had much influence over Bush's cabinet appointments, but they may well have significant sway in the hiring of second- and third-tier officials. These are the people who get their hands dirty on policy details, and can deliver the goodies to the corporate paymasters.

More ceremonial posts are being parceled out with a machine-like efficiency to high donors and top fundraisers.

Inaugural Committee Co-Chairs Bill and Kathy DeWitt and Mercer and Gabrielle Reynolds come from the Cincinnati-based investment firm Reynolds, DeWitt and Company. Bill

DeWitt and Gabrielle Reynolds were co-chairs of the Ohio Bush-Cheney Finance Committee. Other members of the inaugural committee sport similar resumes.

Following in the Clinton-Gore footsteps, Bush-Cheney are soliciting private funds for the inauguration. While Clinton-Gore at least restricted the donations to $100 or less, however, Bush-Cheney are banking on major donors. More than 50 individuals have each contributed $100,000 or more to the inauguration committee.

Bush's economic summit, held earlier this month in Austin, was actually a get-together with business leaders. The Austin meeting featured 36 top corporate executives, including such major Republican donors as Kenneth Lay of Enron, John T. Chambers of Cisco and Michael Dell of Dell Computer.

As you would imagine, this turn of events has corporate America dancing in the streets. "They are happy, certainly," Jim Albertine, president of the American League of Lobbyists, told the *Boston Globe*, speaking of his association's members. "There is a strong belief that a lot of things will be reopened."

The Wartime Opportunists

September 25, 2001

Make way for the wartime opportunists.

Corporate interests and their proxies are looking to exploit the September 11 tragedy to advance a self-serving agenda that has nothing to do with national security and everything to do with corporate profits and dangerous ideologies.

Fast track and the Free Trade Area of the Americas. A corporate tax cut. Oil drilling in Alaska. Star Wars. These are some of the preposterous "solutions" and responses to the terror attack offered by corporate mouthpieces.

No one has been more shameless in linking their agenda to the terror attack than U.S. Trade Representative Robert Zoellick. Writing in the Washington Post last week, Zoellick proclaimed that granting fast-track trade negotiating authority to the president—to assist with the ramming through Congress of a Free Trade Area of the Americas, designed to expand NAFTA to all of the Americas, among other nefarious ends— was the best way to respond to the September 11 tragedy.

"Earlier enemies learned that America is the arsenal of democracy," Zoellick wrote, "Today's enemies will learn that America is the economic engine for freedom, opportunity and development. To that end, U.S. leadership in promoting the international economic and trading system is vital. Trade is about more than economic efficiency. It promotes the values at the heart of this protracted struggle."

No explanation from Zoellick about how adopting a procedural rule designed to limit Congressional debate on controversial trade agreements advances the democratic and rule-of-law values he says the United States must now project.

The administration has identified fast track as one of the handful of legislative priorities it hopes to see Congress enact this year.

Getting fast track passed isn't big business's only priority for the shrinking legislative calendar. The Fortune 500 has been whimpering since George Bush was elected president and top administration officials told the business community to silence their demand for corporate tax cuts until after passage of the inequality-increasing personal income tax cut.

Even before the September 11 attack, business interests and the anti-tax ideologues were increasingly making noise that corporate tax cuts were the solution to the coming recession.

Now they are beginning to argue that capital gains tax cuts and corporate tax breaks are America's patriotic duty.

In releasing a study purporting to explain how a capital gains cut would spur economic growth, the National Taxpayers Union (NTU) touted a capital gains tax cut—a tax break that exclusively benefits the wealthy—as an anti-terrorism initiative. "By reducing the rate at which capital gains are taxed, President Bush and Congress could help revitalize the sagging economy and bring new revenues to Washington—decidedly aiding our war against terrorism," said NTU director of congressional relations Eric Schlecht.

Not wishing to be outdone, Senator Frank Murkowski, R-Alaska, didn't wait long to explain how the terror attack makes it imperative to open up the Arctic National Wildlife Refuge (ANWR). "There is no doubt that at this time of national emergency, an expedited energy-security bill must be considered," the Alaska senator announced last week. "Opening ANWR will be a central element in finally reducing this country's dangerous overdependence on unstable foreign sources of energy," he said.

Neither Murkowski nor the oil companies pushing for opening ANWR have ever been able to offer a coherent explanation of how using up U.S. oil reserves heightens energy security. Security rests in maintaining the reserves. Real energy security and independence can only come from renewables (particularly solar and wind)—where the supply is plentiful and infinitely renewing. Only a failure of public and private investment leaves the country (and the world) unable to harvest renewable energy efficiently.

And, of course, the purveyors of Star Wars couldn't let the opportunity pass them by. The Center for Security Policy—the center of a web of defense industry-backed think tanks and organizations pushing for a National Missile Defense program—urged President Bush in advance of his address to Congress to announce that "this Administration will use every tool at its disposal to ensure that the resources and latitude needed to develop and deploy missile defenses are made available."

A missile defense system—even if it overcame the technical obstacles which have so far proved insurmountable, after billions spent—would have done nothing to stop the September 11 attack. Nor would it do anything to stop any other conceivable terrorist attack on the United States, none of which might involve missile delivery systems.

Opportunism and cynical manipulation of tragedy are nothing new in Washington. But the proposals to exploit the September 11 tragedy for narrow corporate aims mark a new low.

The United States is emerging from a national mourning period. Now is the time to proceed with caution and care, as the nation seeks to address legitimate security concerns (e.g., airport security) and tend to victims of the attack. It is no time to rush through proposals on matters essentially unrelated to the attack, especially damaging and foolhardy proposals that have been unable to win popular or Congressional support when the public has had a chance to consider them dispassionately, and on the merits.

The Cipro Rip-Off
and the Public Health

November 8, 2001

Confronted with the prospect of bioterrorism on a massive scale, the Bush administration and the pharmaceutical industry have colluded to protect patent monopolies rather than the public health.

When the anthrax scare first hit, Cipro was understood to be the drug of choice for treatment. Secretary of Health and Human Services Tommy Thompson said he wanted a stockpile adequate to treat 10 million exposed persons. That meant he needed 1.2 billion Cipro pills (the treatment regimen is two pills for 60 days). Bayer, which holds the disputed patent rights to Cipro in the United States, could not meet that demand in a timely fashion.

For the drugs it was able to supply, Bayer was charging the government $1.89 per pill. The drugstore price was more than $4.50. Indian companies sell a generic version of the same drug for less than 20 cents.

The U.S. government has authority, under existing law, to license generic companies to make on-patent drugs for sale to the government. Those companies could have met supply needs that Bayer was not and is not able to satisfy. Generic competition might also have helped bring prices down, though it is unclear exactly what the government would have to pay Bayer if it bought generic versions of Cipro.

But the Bush administration chose not to exercise this authority. Pharmaceutical industry monopolistic patent protections are so sacrosanct, the administration decided, that even urgent U.S. public health needs do not merit any limitation on patent monopolies.

The administration was motivated in significant part by fear that if it authorized generic production in the United States for Cipro, it would undermine its hand in negotiations at the

World Trade Organization (WTO) meeting in Qatar. There, African and other poor countries are asking for a declaration that the WTO's intellectual property rules not be interpreted in ways that undermine efforts to advance public health. Above all, they want to clarify their existing right under WTO rules to authorize generic production of on-patent drugs (a practice known as compulsory licensing). The United States, pathetically, is opposing this effort.

With the spotlight shining on Bayer's price-gouging for Cipro, the Department of Health and Human Services had to take action. It cut a deal with the company to lower Cipro prices, agreeing on a price tag of 95 cents a pill. That supposedly cut-rate price turns out to be twice what the same government, indeed the same government agency, pays the same company for the same drug under another program.

But though inadequate, the price reduction did reflect the U.S. government's negotiating leverage—leverage that was enhanced by the fact that the government had the authority to turn to generic manufacturers if Bayer refused to cut a deal.

What hypocrisy! At the same time as it leveraged the

threat of a compulsory license, the administration is working feverishly in diverse fora—including the WTO and the Free Trade Area of the Americas negotiations—to limit poor countries' effective ability to do compulsory licensing.

It is time to reverse course, and for citizens to demand the government prioritize public health over corporate profit.

In the United States, it is unclear how much Cipro the government should stockpile as a public health measure. Other, off-patent antibiotics may be superior and are cheaper. These other drugs may or may not be effective against all strains of anthrax. What is clear is that intellectual property issues should have no impact on public health judgments made in this context.

Representative Sherrod Brown has introduced legislation, H.R. 3235, the Public Health Emergency Medicines Act, that would reiterate the government's ability to do compulsory licensing in case of public health emergency (the government currently has this right, without regard to situation of national emergency) and establish that compensation paid to patent holders should be "reasonable." It lists a variety of criteria to determine reasonability, including how much the patent holder invested and risked in the drug's development, and how significant the government contribution was to the drug's research and development. It also would permit the government to authorize generic producers to manufacture on-patent drugs in the United States for export to countries undergoing public health emergencies. The Public Health Emergency Medicines Act should quickly become law.

In international treaty negotiations, it is time for the United States to stop identifying its interests only with those of the brand-name drug manufacturers. The government should immediately cease its shameful opposition to a declaration that the WTO intellectual property agreement should not hinder developing country measures to protect public health. It should agree to accept the few needed clarifications to WTO rules to make compulsory licensing workable in poor countries over the long haul. It should end its sneaky efforts in the Free Trade Area of the Americas and other negotiations to impose technical rules that would impede compulsory licensing. And Congress should deny the administration the fast-track authority it seeks to facilitate negotiation of more trade rules enhancing the brand-name drug companies' monopoly power.

Stealing Money From Kids

January 28, 2003

If there's one thing that brings together the right and the left, and citizens and corporations, it is the importance of education—for stimulating the intellect, developing a moral sensibility, enhancing the civic culture, enabling a skilled workforce and creating a sense of community.

The question is: Who's willing to pay?

Not big corporations.

They instead demand cities and states offer tax breaks before they will invest in new plants and facilities. Those tax breaks, frequently in the form of property tax abatements or what is called tax increment financing (TIF, a long-term diversion of certain areas' property taxes to corporations investing in those areas), deprive schools of money.

Property tax breaks often directly siphon money away from schools, which rely heavily on property taxes as a revenue source. According to "Protecting Public Education From Tax Giveaways to Corporations," a report issued last week by the National Education Association (NEA), local property taxes constitute 65 percent of all local education funding, and 29 percent of all school funding, including local, state and federal contributions.

Property tax abatements and TIF districts cost schools hundreds of millions of dollars a year, at least.

Case studies in the NEA report, which was conducted by Good Jobs First, the leading organization studying state and local business subsidies, show that abatements and TIF districts cost schools in Texas $52 million a year. Montana schools lose $16 million a year in revenues to business tax subsidies. Abatements and TIF reduced or diverted property tax revenue for Ohio schools by $102 million in 1999.

Poor reporting rules and the diversity of jurisdictions and tax revenues make it almost impossible to determine a total cost to schools from business tax breaks.

However, some estimates have tagged the cost of local and state subsidies to business as high as $50 billion annually. This is an estimate of the total cost, not just the amount borne by schools, and some states reimburse schools, in whole or part, for revenues foregone due to property tax breaks.

The NEA report offers three recommendations to redress the problem highlighted by the study. First, there should be improved disclosure of subsidies and enforcement of conditions attached to subsidies. Second, local school boards should have a formal say—up to and including veto power—over subsidy decisions. Third, states should prohibit the abatement or diversion of the school portion of property taxes.

This all seems logical enough to us.

What the report did not do was suggest what corporations' role should be in these matters. Since corporations drive the "bidding for business" game, this is an important question.

Since companies so heavily emphasize the importance of a skilled workforce, shouldn't corporations simply be willing not to ask for property tax abatements?

We decided to call up the U.S. Chamber of Commerce and find out.

We asked Marty Regalia, the Chamber's chief economist: In light of the impact on schools, should companies stop seeking tax breaks from cities and states?

That proposal, he said, is "blatantly un-American." (Yes, they really talk this way at the Chamber.)

No one forces cities and states to give tax breaks, he said. They are competing for a benefit—new investment—and they choose to enter the competition. If they think it is a bad deal, they are free not to offer tax breaks. "Local communities do not give away [tax breaks] at gunpoint," he said.

There is some truth to Regalia's point that cities and states are free to decline to offer tax benefits.

The problem, though, is not just that most government

officials are spineless and/or indentured to business, but that there is an inherent difference in bargaining power between government and business. The companies have the power to decide where to locate. And even though most threats to move factories or offices are bluffs, in some cases, a tax break may influence a decision to locate in this town or the one next door.

However, property tax breaks and benefits virtually never determine whether or not a company of any size is going to undertake a new investment.

In the bigger picture, and based on the rules of the game, the outcome is always the same: the cities and states collectively lose tax revenues, the investing company always saves money that it would have been willing to pay in taxes on investments it would have made anyway.

This all comes at the expense of education, among other important government spending priorities.

The tax breaks are taking money from kids as sure as the schoolyard bully stealing classmates' lunch money—just on a scale so large that few have been willing to call it by name.

Too Much

February 25, 2003

For almost two years now, we have covered the Bush White House with astonishment.

We are astonished by the simple fact that this President, with such strong ties to the corporate establishment, has for two years sailed smoothly through our democratic waters, at a time of rising popular discontent, unemployment, corporate scandals, national security disasters, and most recently, gasoline above $2 a gallon.

How does he do it?

First and foremost is the failure of the political opposition.

The Republicans are bought and paid for.

The leadership of the Democratic Party is timid, bought and paid for.

So, with no effective opposition in Washington, the President gets a free ride.

Unless the press puts his feet to the fire.

Now, the Bush White House press operatives are, if anything, professionals at ducking, banning, evading and dodging.

President Bush has given the fewest number of press conferences of any president in recent years.

The President's press office is perhaps one of the best in recent years, if you define its job as keeping reporters at bay.

How do they do it?

Well, first, they keep out reporters who they dislike.

Remember Sarah McClendon? She has been a thorn in the side of presidents since Franklin Delano Roosevelt. She passed away last month. Ari Fleischer went to her memorial service.

For more than 60 years, Sarah McClendon had unfettered access to White House press briefings with her White House press pass.

But the Bush White House wanted no part of her, so they

refused to renew her press pass in June 2001, according to John Hurley, a colleague who still runs the McClendon Study Group.

We were denied access to the White House for a number of months in 2001—we were told we told it was about "national security."

Translate—we don't like your penchant for asking about corporate power.

Then, when we beat the rap, we were told that there was no way that we were going to get a White House press pass.

Why? Because we didn't meet the criteria.

What are the criteria, we asked?

After months of no answer, we were told the criteria are:

You have to be assigned to cover the White House daily. Check.

You are accredited by the House and Senate gallery. Check.

You are willing to undergo the required Secret Service background investigation. Check.

Check, check and check.

So, we meet all the criteria.

Why don't we get a pass?

More months have passed. Still no answer.

But we are welcome at the White House, we are told, no problem, just call ahead every day so that we can clear you in. No problem.

So, we call ahead every day, and we get cleared in.

Unless the day is like yesterday, when we e-mailed our handler at the White House to get cleared in, are e-mailed back telling us that we were cleared in, but then when we get to the White House, we are told we are not cleared in. Sorry. You'll have to wait until you are cleared in.

Yesterday, Ari Fleischer's press briefing was scheduled at 12:15. Ari starts his press briefing then. We are left waiting at the White House gate until 12:40. We get in. Take a seat, and Ari gets to us, and skips over us.

So, first they ban you.

Then they leave you stewing at the gate.

Then they skip over you.

And yesterday is not the first time we've been through that scenario.

If you get in, and if Ari calls on you, he limits the number of questions you get.

The Fox News reporter gets four, five or six a day. We get zero, one or two.

If Ari takes your question, he more often than not evades the question.

And if pressed, he dodges the question.

Like today. Here's the exchange:

Question: Ari, two things.

Ari Fleischer: We're going to—the one question rule has to be in effect because I'm going to have to be in the Oval Office at 1:05 p.m. [Unless you're from Fox News.]

Question: Okay. The Washington Post reported yesterday on its front page that "many people in the world increasingly think that President Bush is a greater threat to world peace than Iraqi President Saddam Hussein." Why do you think that millions of people around the world hold that view?

Fleischer: I don't think that—number one, the President is going to do what he thinks is right representing the American people ...

Question: But why do you think millions of people hold that view?

Ari Fleischer: I'm not in a position to judge it ...

This is typical Fleischer. He first starts talking about the American people—the question was about people overseas. Then when pressed, he says—I'm not in a position to judge it. Evade and dodge.

Toward the end of the press conference today, a reporter from South America raises the question of President Bush bribing foreign governments to side with the United States against the will of their own people on war with Iraq.

This is obviously happening, and has been reported just today by the Associated Press and *USA Today*, among others. The United States is sending billions of taxpayer dollars to countries like Spain and Turkey, where more than 90 percent of the people oppose the war. We bribe their governments to turn against the will of their own people.

And the President talks about exporting democracy?

Anyway, the South American journalist wanted to know whether the President was seeking to buy the vote of Mexico in the United Nation's Security Council's upcoming vote on war in Iraq by promising some "sort of immigration agreements like amnesty or [a] guest worker program."

"Think about the implications of what you're saying," Fleischer responds. "You're saying that the leaders of other nations are buyable."

Even for the laid back White House press corps, this was too much.

They break out in laughter. Ari walks out.

End of press conference.

Crooks

July 8, 2003

The two major political parties are crooked.

Without shame, they take big money from criminals.

Corporate Crime Reporter last week released a report documenting $9.3 million given by convicted criminals to the Democrats and the Republicans in the 2002 election cycle. (See the full report, "Dirty Money: Corporate Criminal Donations to the Two Major Parties," at www.corporatecrimereporter.com)

The Democrats took $2.1 million of the dirty money, the Republicans took $7.2 million.

Terry McAuliffe, the chairman of the Democratic National Committee, condemns President Bush for his "inability to stand up to corporate criminals."

Et tu, Terry?

President Bush talks a tough line on corporate crime, but then pockets millions from the crooks and proceeds to dismantle the enforcement agencies that would crack down on the most serious of those crimes.

Both Deborah DeShong, communications director of the Democratic National Committee, and Christine Iverson, press secretary for the Republican National Committee, did not return calls seeking comment on this story.

Probably the right move.

How can a political party defend taking money from convicted corporate criminals?

It is indefensible.

The Dirty Money report found that 31 major convicted corporations gave the $9.3 million to the two political parties in the 2002 election cycle.

(These soft money contributions will be prohibited in future elections, due to the McCain-Feingold campaign finance reform legislation. However, corporate criminal campaign funding will still flow from company PACs, company executives' hard money contributions and burgeoning "527" issue committees, and to state parties.)

Archer Daniels Midland—ADM—tops the list of criminals that gave money to the parties.

ADM pled guilty in 1996 to one of the largest antitrust crimes ever. The company paid a $100 million criminal fine—at the time, the largest criminal antitrust fine ever.

The company was convicted of engaging in conspiracies to fix prices, to eliminate competition, and to allocate sales in the lysine and citric acid markets worldwide.

So, here we have a major American corporation, convicted of an egregious antitrust crime that cost us all tens of millions of dollars.

And it turns around and freely gives $1.7 million to Democrats and Republicans—in just the last two years.

And the two major political parties are not ashamed.

They do not blush.

They do not care.

Because it is apparently okay in Washington to take money from convicted corporate criminals.

The second largest corporate criminal donor is Pfizer, the pharmaceutical giant, the maker of Lipitor, and Viagra and Zoloft.

In 1999, Pfizer pled guilty to fixing prices in the food additives industry. The company paid $20 million in fines.

No free market philosophy for ADM and Pfizer—when in doubt, fix prices.

In the last two years, Pfizer gave $1.1 million to the Democrats and Republicans. Convicted criminal.

The parties looked the other way.

Chevron was convicted in 1992 of environmental crimes and paid a $6.5 million criminal fine. Chevron gave $875,400 in the 2002 election cycle to both parties.

Grumman, which was convicted in 1990 of false statements—lying—gave $741,250 to both political parties in the most recent election cycle.

And American Airlines, convicted in 2000 of illegal storage of hazardous waste at Miami airport, paid a fine of $8 million, and then turned around and donated $655,593 to the Democrats and Republicans.

Where is Ann Coulter?

Where is Rush Limbaugh?

Where is Bill Bennett?

Where is Hannity and where is Colmes?

Where are the conservative drumbeaters, condemning criminality at every turn?

Why aren't they raving about the convicted criminals in our midst?

These convicted criminals are companies with massive resources, with the ability to manipulate the system to avoid the criminal penalty even when they are caught red-handed.

Yet defying the odds, these companies were caught red-handed and they were forced to plead guilty to serious crimes.

Last year, during the height of the corporate crime wave, scores of lawmakers felt it necessary to give back to Enron PACs or to Enron executives money that had been donated to their campaigns.

These politicians felt a sense of shame—especially since the television cameras were focused non-stop on the issue—until Bush moved the spotlight to Iraq.

Here was Enron, a runaway corporation that epitomized the fast and loose business ethics of recent years.

That runaway corporation crashed, leaving thousands unemployed and without pensions. Ever since, Enron executives are being indicted left and right.

And so, scores of public officials who had financially benefited from Enron's largesse felt a sense of shame, and felt threatened by an angry public, so they decided to give the money back to Enron—or better yet, to donate it to charity.

It was the right thing to do.

Politicians should not take money from crooked companies, or crooked executives, or PACs set up by crooked companies.

But Enron has not been indicted.

Enron is not a convicted corporation.

And yet scores of politicians, because of the political heat, because of the scorching white glare of publicity, decided that Enron money was too hot to handle.

But what about the convicted corporations that every year donate millions to both political parties?

We call upon the Democratic and Republican parties to get rid of this dirty money.

It is tainted money.

It is criminal money.

Give it up.

Terry Gross, Grover Norquist and the Holocaust

October 7, 2003

Terry Gross has a syndicated show on National Public Radio. It's called "Fresh Air."

As a guest last week, Gross had on Grover Norquist, the head of Americans for Tax Reform and the reputed architect of President Bush's tax cuts.

One of Terry Gross' first questions to Grover Norquist was this one:

"Now the Bush tax cuts would cost us about $1.1 trillion over the next 10 years, and we're going to be hundreds of billions of dollars in debt. At the same time, the president wants $87 billion to rebuild Iraq and Afghanistan. Do you think we're in a tough spot, needing a lot of money, to rebuild those two countries at the same time that we're cutting taxes?

And here's Grover Norquist's answer:

"Well, there's a very interesting use of the word 'we.' Every time you use the word 'we,' you meant the government, and I tend to use the word 'we' to mean the American people and to speak of the government as the government. So when the government doesn't take as much of your money next year as it did last year, we have more money. The government has a lower tax rate, and depending on economic growth, may have more or less money, but we, the people, have more money. So it is a good thing for us to have lower taxes."

Wow, Grover—we can't use the word "we" anymore to refer to a political entity called the government?

What do you propose we replace the word "we" with in the following, Grover?

"We the people of the United States, in order to form a more perfect union, establish justice, insure domestic tranquility, provide for the common defense, promote general welfare, and secure the blessing of liberty to ourselves and our posterity, do ordain and establish this Constitution for the United States of America."

Terry Gross then moves on to the estate tax. Here's the back and forth:

Terry Gross: The estate tax is only paid by somebody who gets over $2 million in inheritance. So, you know, when you get out of poverty and you cross that line which is—What is it, like, $18,000 or something that's officially poverty line?

Grover Norquist: Depends on how many kids you have. Yeah.

Terry Gross: Right. OK. So when you cross that, maybe you're making, like, $20,000 or something. That's not going to help you with the estate tax. I mean, you're talking about $2 million. That's a line people don't cross a lot. That's—I don't think that's...

Grover Norquist: Yeah, the good news about the move to abolish the death tax, the tax where they come and look at how much money you've got when you die, how much gold is in your teeth and they want half of it, is that—you're right, there's an exemption for—I don't know—maybe a million dollars now, and it's scheduled to go up a little bit. However, 70 percent of the American people want to abolish that tax. Congress, the House and Senate, have three times voted to abolish it. The president supports abolishing it, so that tax is going to be abolished. I think it speaks very much to the health of the nation that 70-plus percent of Americans want to abolish the death tax, because they see it as fundamentally unjust. The argument that some who played at the politics of hate and envy and class division will say, 'Yes, well, that's only 2 percent,' or as people get richer 5 percent in the near future of Americans likely to have to pay that tax.

I mean, that's the morality of the Holocaust. 'Well, it's only a small percentage,' you know. 'I mean, it's not you, it's somebody else.'

And this country, people who may not make earning a lot

of money the centerpiece of their lives, they may have other things to focus on, they just say it's not just. If you've paid taxes on your income once, the government should leave you alone. Shouldn't come back and try and tax you again.

Terry Gross: Excuse me. Excuse me one second. Did you just...

Grover Norquist: Yeah?

Terry Gross: compare the estate tax with the Holocaust?

Grover Norquist: No, the morality that says it's OK to do something to do a group because they're a small percentage of the population is the morality that says that the Holocaust is OK because they didn't target everybody, just a small percentage. What are you worried about? It's not you. It's not you. It's them. And arguing that it's OK to loot some group because it's them, or kill some group because it's them and because it's a small number, that has no place in a democratic society that treats people equally. The government's going to do something to or for us, it should treat us all equally."

Terry Gross: So you see taxes as being the way they are now terrible discrimination against the wealthy comparable to the kind of discrimination of, say, the Holocaust?

Grover Norquist: Well, what you pick—you can use different rhetoric or different points for different purposes, and I would argue that those who say, 'Don't let this bother you; I'm only doing it'—I, the government. The government is only doing it to a small percentage of the population. That is very wrong. And it's immoral. They should treat everybody the same. They shouldn't be shooting anyone, and they shouldn't be taking half of anybody's income or wealth when they die."

First of all, Grover, the morality underpinning the estate tax is the not same as the "morality" underpinning the holocaust.

The holocaust was mass killing driven by a racist ideology. There is no morality there.

The estate tax is a moral tax—taxing the wealth of the

super-rich to help the not so super-rich—it's called progressive taxation.

According to Bill Gates Sr. and Chuck Collins of the group Responsible Wealth, nearly half of all estate taxes are paid by the wealthiest 0.1 percent of the American population—a few thousand families each year.

In 2001, Gates was the lead signer on Responsible Wealth's Call to Preserve the Estate Tax, which was signed by over 1,000 wealthy people personally affected by the estate tax—including George Soros, Ted Turner, and David Rockefeller Jr. He points out that since it was enacted in 1916, the estate tax has helped to limit the concentration of wealth, making it easier for Americans to educate themselves, innovate, build new businesses, and prosper.

Gates also points out that while there is no question that "some people accumulate great wealth through hard work, intelligence, creativity, and sacrifice" it is equally important to acknowledge "the influence of other factors, such as luck, privilege, other people's efforts, and society's investment in the creation of individual wealth such as a patent system, enforceable contracts, open courts, property ownership records, protection against crime and external threats, and public education."

The father of the man with the billions understands the word "we."

Get it, Grover?

Say No to Silicone

Eleven years ago, the U.S. Food and Drug Administration announced it was pulling silicone breast implants from the market, leaving them available only to breast cancer survivors who needed them for reconstruction or to women enrolled in limited clinical studies.

The reason for the action, announced then-FDA Commissioner David Kessler, was that, under the law, "these types of products have to be shown by their manufacturer to be safe and effective before they may be distributed and used. Some people argue that the devices have to be proven unsafe before the FDA can act to protect patients against their use. This is not so. The burden of proof is an affirmative one and it rests with the manufacturer. In this instance, the manufacturers have not shown these devices to be safe."

Although silicone breast implants had been on the market for three decades, Kessler said, "the list of unanswered questions is long."

"We do not know how long these devices will last," he said.

"We know that some of these implants will rupture, but we don't know how many of them will rupture," he pointed out.

And, he said, "We don't know whether there is any link between the implants and immune-related disorders and other systemic diseases."

"Until these basic questions are satisfactorily answered, we cannot approve these devices."

Fast forward to the present.

Dow Corning, the leading manufacturer of silicone implants more than a decade ago, is in bankruptcy.

Inamed, a California-based company, is now seeking marketing authorization from the FDA for silicone breast implants.

More than a decade has passed since the FDA restricted

sales of silicone implants, but Inamed only submitted to FDA three years worth of data from a study projected to continue for 10 years. The company sells silicone implants in Europe and more than 60 countries worldwide, but it hasn't collected any safety information from women in those countries that is of high enough quality to submit to FDA.

As a result, we still don't know the answers to many of the questions Kessler identified, and most of what we do know is frightening.

What we do know is that painful breast hardening which can lead to deformity, dead tissue, loss of nipple sensation, infections and rashes are common complications from silicone implants.

We know that rupture rates leading silicone to spread throughout the body are extremely high over the long term—occurring in more than half or two thirds of women after 10 years, according to two studies.

We don't know whether there is any link between the implants and immune-related disorders and other systemic diseases, though there is worrying evidence that they do.

We started to ask Inamed spokesperson Peter Nicholson about these matters, but he'd only say that the data Inamed submitted to the FDA was available on the web, and the company would not be commenting further.

Inamed's data are indeed striking.

Even though the company reported on only three year's test results, the numbers show significant short-term problems. After just three years, one in five augmentation patients and almost half of reconstruction patients required additional surgeries.

Inamed's data did not show particularly high rupture rates during the three-year period of study—in no small part because it only provided MRIs to about a third of the women in the study, and silicone rupture can only be detected through MRIs.

Inamed's data were replete with other flaws. For example,

the company misleadingly claimed a low incidence of lactation problems, by comparing the incidence of problems to the overall population of women receiving augmentation, not just those who tried to breastfeed.

These and other problems were pointed out by advocacy groups at an FDA advisory committee hearing convened last month to issue a recommendation on whether Inamed's marketing application should be approved.

The advisory committee also heard heart-wrenching testimony from more than two dozen women with silicone implants. They described the extreme pain and life-changing problems they have suffered as a result of silicone implants in terms that could fail to move only those with hardened hearts. And several highlighted an important economic component—health insurance plans generally do not cover surgeries to remove implants for augmentation patients, placing a huge financial burden on sick women.

Nonetheless, the advisory panel, a quarter of whom are plastic surgeons, and at least one of whom was swayed by empty promises from Inamed to do ongoing follow-up research, voted 9-6 to recommend the FDA approve Inamed's request.

The failure for a larger majority to support the application leaves it awkward for FDA to recommend approval.

Inamed's chances of approval worsened last week, when Dr. Thomas Whalen, the non-voting chair of the advisory panel, in a highly unusual move, sent a letter to FDA commissioner Mark McClellan. Whalen called the panel decision "misguided," emphasizing the lack of data on long-term safety. He felt "morally compelled" to urge the FDA to deny approval, he told reporters.

Now the decision rests with FDA Commissioner Mark McClellan.

The law hasn't changed since the time the FDA ordered silicone implants off the market. The agency faces the same choice it faced in 1992, with little new information—and much of the recent information indicating the implants' hazards.

If the FDA upholds its obligation under the law to approve products only that afford "a reasonable assurance of safety," it has no choice but to deny approval.

You can help influence the decision. Send a message to FDA Commissioner McClellan urging him not to approve Inamed's application. You can do this from the website of the Command Trust Network, an information clearinghouse on implants, at: <http://www.commandtrust.org>.

PART THREE

GLOBAL DOMINATION

What is perhaps most distinctive about the current epoch of corporate globalization is not the increasing amount of international trade, skyrocketing rates of cross-border investments, or even the ability of manufacturers to quickly shift production from one site to another in search of lower wages, laxer environmental rules, lower taxes or other corporate perks. Perhaps the crucial unique feature of the current period is the effort through international public institutions to strip countries of their ability to choose their own public policies.

Through the structural adjustment programs of the International Monetary Fund (IMF) and World Bank, and the extensive and intrusive rules of the World Trade Organization (WTO), multinational corporations seek to force countries around the globe to adhere to a single economic model, to harmonize their rules and regulations to the corporate behemoths' liking, to guarantee equal protection to foreign investors.

These are life-and-death matters. When the IMF and World Bank require countries to charge fees for access to basic healthcare, people in poor countries go without care. When WTO rules are invoked to pressure Guatemala to abandon labeling rules for infant formula, mothers are lured to use formula instead of healthier breastmilk. When the IMF's shock therapy sends the Russian economy into a tailspin, the number of Russians in poverty rises from two million to more than 50 million. Nowhere are the stakes higher than in the area of access to essential medicines. The global pharmaceutical industry has tried to use the intellectual property rules of the WTO and other international agreements to block developing countries from taking steps to make affordable, generic medicines available.

With more than 25 million people in Africa infected with HIV/AIDS, and the pandemic spreading quickly throughout the developing world, making affordable treatments available is a humanitarian imperative. Drug cocktails allow many people in the United States and rich countries with HIV/AIDS to survive. In the United States, those cocktails cost more than $10,000 a year, far beyond the reach of the citizens in African countries where per capita incomes may be a few hundred dollars a year.

Until recently, AIDS drugs prices in developing countries were roughly the same as in the United States. But in recent years, generic competition has lowered the poor country price of brand-name products in some cases to as low as $500 a year. Generic manufacturers can make AIDS cocktails for $140 a year.

The high price of medicines has almost nothing to do with the cost of manufacturing, and everything to do with the monopolies conferred by patents. WTO rules require all members to issue patents for pharmaceuticals, but include safeguards to permit early introduction of generic competition to satisfy public health needs. If the safeguards are to mean anything, they should be used to address the world's worst pandemic since the Black Death—yet Big Pharma and the U.S. government have conspired to deter developing countries from exercising the flexibilities in the WTO agreement.

The Drug Lords Defeated

September 24, 1999

Sometimes, the multinationals lose.

Last week, the United States government announced that it will stop bullying South Africa to abandon efforts to make essential medicines available to its population.

Chalk up a win for public health—thousands of lives may be saved as a result of the new U.S. policy—and a loss for the pharmaceutical industry. The industry had relied on the U.S. Trade Representative to act as its proxy in pressuring South Africa to abandon policies that the drug companies believe to be contrary to their interests.

As is almost always the case, this defeat of corporate interests is primarily attributable to one thing: citizen pressure.

In this instance, the reversal of U.S. policy came as a direct result of a courageous and strategically savvy campaign conducted by AIDS activists.

They forced the issue on to the national political scene and into the national media in June, when they interrupted Al Gore's announcement that he was running for president.

Chanting "Gore's Greed Kills" and "AIDS drugs for Africa," the protesters dogged Gore at various other public events for a three-month period.

Two million people die annually from AIDS-related causes, the overwhelming majority in the Third World, and the number is skyrocketing. Drug treatments that enable many people with AIDS in industrialized countries to survive are priced out of reach of all but a tiny number of HIV-positive people in the Third World. When South Africa and other Third World countries have sought to take measures to reduce the price of AIDS and other essential medicines, the U.S. government has threatened trade and other sanctions to block them.

Apparently none of this was newsworthy for the major U.S. media.

But the media did find that disruptions of Gore's speeches merited coverage, and so the vice president's staff quickly moved to make the protests stop.

The protesters targeted Gore because he has co-chaired (along with current South African President Thabo Mbeki) the U.S.-South Africa binational commission, the vehicle through which the U.S. government applied its pressure on South Africa. They also picked Gore because they recognized that he was vulnerable to negative publicity.

The result of the activist campaign was an announcement by the U.S. Trade Representative and the South African government that the U.S. government would cease pressuring South Africa on the issues of compulsory licensing and parallel imports. Compulsory licensing enables a government to authorize generic production of a product while it is still on patent, with royalties paid to the patent holder. Parallel imports involves imports of drugs retailed in one country for resale in another, so that the parallel importing country can benefit from lower prices elsewhere in the world.

Through its Medicines Act, South Africa has sought to make use of these two tools. With as many as one in six South African adults HIV positive, AIDS drugs are a top candidate for compulsory licensing and parallel imports.

Since compulsory licensing can drop the price of drugs by 75 percent or more, if South Africa is able to proceed with its plans (it still must resolve a domestic lawsuit challenging the law which was filed by dozens of multinational pharmaceutical companies), many people are likely to gain access to life-saving medicines who would otherwise go without.

There apparently was no written agreement between the United States and South Africa, or if there was the two governments are refusing to release it, but it appears to represent a total U.S. capitulation. South Africa appears to have made no concessions, promising only to adhere to its obligations under the World Trade Organization (which permits compulsory licensing and parallel imports)—a commitment it had already made repeatedly.

As important as it is, this access-to-medicines victory is only partial, even leaving aside broader questions about maintaining adequate health care systems in developing countries, say, or finding a cure for AIDS.

The U.S. agreement applies only to South Africa. It still remains for the U.S. government to declare that other nations can employ compulsory licensing and parallel imports without fear of repercussion.

And there remains the matter of whether the U.S. government will license the patent rights it holds to essential medicines to the World Health Organization, which could then disseminate low-priced versions of the medicines worldwide.

AIDS activists plan to raise these issues at demonstrations in Washington, D.C. on October 6.

But for now, they are entitled to take a couple days and savor a tremendous victory over the powerful pharmaceutical industry.

10 Reasons to Dismantle the WTO

November 23, 1999

Add a new constituency to the long list of World Trade Organization (WTO) critics which already includes consumers, labor, environmentalists, human rights activists, fair trade groups, AIDS activists, animal protection organizations, those concerned with Third World development, religious communities and women's organizations. The latest set of critics includes WTO backers and even the WTO itself.

As the WTO faces crystallized global opposition—to be manifested in massive street demonstrations and colorful protests in Seattle, where the WTO will hold its Third Ministerial meeting from November 30 to December 3—the global trade agency and its strongest proponents veer between a shrill defensiveness and the much more effective strategy of admitting shortcomings and trumpeting the need for reform.

WTO critics now face a perilous moment. They must not be distracted by illusory or cosmetic reform proposals, nor by even more substantive proposals for changing the WTO—should they ever emerge from the institution or its powerful rich country members. Instead, they should unite around an uncompromising demand to dismantle the WTO and its corporate-created rules.

Here are 10 reasons why:

1. The WTO prioritizes trade and commercial considerations over all other values. WTO rules generally require domestic laws, rules and regulations designed to further worker, consumer, environmental, health, safety, human rights, animal protection or other non-commercial interests to be undertaken in the "least trade restrictive" fashion possible—almost never is trade subordinated to these noncommercial concerns.

2. The WTO undermines democracy. Its rules drastically shrink the choices available to democratically controlled governments, with violations potentially punished with harsh

penalties. The WTO actually touts this overriding of domestic decisions about how economies should be organized and corporations controlled. "Under WTO rules, once a commitment has been made to liberalize a sector of trade, it is difficult to reverse," the WTO says in a paper on the benefits of the organization which is published on its web site. "Quite often, governments use the WTO as a welcome external constraint on their policies: 'we can't do this because it would violate the WTO agreements.'"

3. The WTO does not just regulate, it actively promotes, global trade. Its rules are biased to facilitate global commerce at the expense of efforts to promote local economic development and policies that move communities, countries and regions in the direction of greater self-reliance.

4. The WTO hurts the Third World. WTO rules force Third World countries to open their markets to rich country multinationals, and abandon efforts to protect infant domestic industries. In agriculture, the opening to foreign imports, soon to be imposed on developing countries, will catalyze a massive social dislocation of many millions of rural people.

5. The WTO eviscerates the Precautionary Principle. WTO rules generally block countries from acting in response to potential risk—requiring a probability before governments can move to resolve harms to human health or the environment.

6. The WTO squashes diversity. WTO rules establish international health, environmental and other standards as a global ceiling through a process of "harmonization;" countries or even states and cities can only exceed them by overcoming high hurdles.

7. The WTO operates in secrecy. Its tribunals rule on the "legality" of nations' laws, but carry out their work behind closed doors.

8. The WTO limits governments' ability to use their purchasing dollar for human rights, environmental, worker rights and other non-commercial purposes. In general, WTO rules

state that governments can make purchases based only on quality and cost considerations.

9. The WTO disallows bans on imports of goods made with child labor. In general, WTO rules do not allow countries to treat products differently based on how they were produced—irrespective of whether made with brutalized child labor, with workers exposed to toxics or with no regard for species protection.

10. The WTO legitimizes life patents. WTO rules permit and in some cases require patents or similar exclusive protections for life forms.

Some of these problems, such as the WTO's penchant for secrecy, could potentially be fixed, but the core problems—prioritization of commercial over other values, the constraints on democratic decision-making and the bias against local economies—cannot, for they are inherent in the WTO itself.

Because of these unfixable problems, the World Trade Organization should be shut down, sooner rather than later.

That doesn't mean interim steps shouldn't be taken. It does mean that beneficial reforms will focus not on adding new areas of competence to the WTO or enhancing its authority, even if the new areas appear desirable (such as labor rights or competition). Instead, the reforms to pursue are those that reduce or limit the WTO's power—for example, by denying it the authority to invalidate laws passed pursuant to international environmental agreements, limiting application of WTO agricultural rules in the Third World, or eliminating certain subject matters (such as essential medicines or life forms) from coverage under the WTO's intellectual property agreement.

These measures are necessary and desirable in their own right, and they would help generate momentum to close down the WTO.

IMF/World Bank:
Stupid, Cruel, Brutal

October 12, 2000

There is no policy of the International Monetary Fund (IMF) and World Bank that is more stupid, cruel and brutal than the insistence that poor countries charge fees for children to attend school and for people to access basic health services.

The IMF and World Bank condition loans to impoverished countries on the adoption of Contract with America-style "structural adjustment" policies. User fees—also known as community financing, cost sharing or cost recovery—are often one part of the structural adjustment policy package.

In passing an appropriations amendment in July that would stop future funding for the IMF and the World Bank if the two lending agencies do not stop imposing user fees for basic healthcare and education services, the U.S. House of Representatives has taken an important step toward ending this callous and wrongheaded policy.

Unfortunately, the Treasury Department, anxious to avoid any appropriations limitations for its IMF and World Bank policy arms, is working to block inclusion of the amendment in the final foreign operations appropriations bill. As administration officials and members of Congress and their staffs negotiate the terms of a final foreign operations appropriations bill, the educational opportunity and health of millions of people in the world's poorest countries hang in the balance.

The evidence accumulated from around the world over the last decade is quite clear. User fees for education lower school attendance rates, especially among young girls. User fees for primary health services deny access to care and preventative treatment for the poor, leading to the spread of unnecessary and preventable death and disease. And user fee "exemptions" for the poor, or sliding payment scales, routinely fail due to administrative problems, corruption, inadequate notice to the poor or other difficulties.

- In Gambia, in primary health care program villages with insecticide provided free of charge, bednet impregnation—for malaria prevention—was five times higher than in villages where charges were introduced. Households consistently cited lack of money as the main reason they chose not to dip bednets.

- Introduction of a 33 cent fee for visits to Kenyan outpatient health centers led to a 52 percent reduction in outpatient visits. After the fee was suspended, visits rose 41 percent. In Papua New Guinea, the introduction of user fees led to a 30 percent decline in outpatient visits. Studies in Niger have found that user fees extend the period that patients wait before seeking outpatient care.

- UNICEF reports that in Malawi, the elimination of modest school fees and uniform requirements in 1994 caused primary enrollment to increase by about 50 percent virtually overnight—from 1.9 million to 2.9 million. The main beneficiaries were girls. Malawi has been able to maintain near full enrollment since that time.

- In India, reports Dr. Vineeta Gupta, general secretary of Insaaf International, a Punjab, India-based organization, a World Bank-inspired system which is supposed to exclude the poor from healthcare charges fails in practice due to corruption and administrative difficulties, denying the poorest Indians access to healthcare services.

The purported logic of education and healthcare user fees is that payments from children's families and sick people will enable government service agencies to provide services to more people.

But this is a twisted rationale, which should be rejected on both principled and practical grounds. As an issue of principle, access to primary education and healthcare is a right that should not be conditioned on ability to pay.

In practical terms, the real-world record shows that user fees deny children educational opportunity and people of all ages access to basic health services. Charges typically generate little revenue in any case. So the ultimate result of user fees is service denial, not expansion.

The IMF/Bank user fee rationalization presents a false choice: even poor country governments have multiple sources of potential revenue there are ways to increase funding for basic services without imposing charges. Most importantly, the real way to free up resources for education and healthcare is for the World Bank and IMF, without delay, to use their existing assets to cancel the debts owed them by poor countries.

There are no significant corporate or monied interests served by the imposition of user fees in desperately poor countries. The IMF and World Bank continue to support them out of a dogmatic commitment to a marketized ideology that refuses to concede to empirical refutation. The Treasury Department is opposing corrective legislation so that it can preserve its control of the IMF and World Bank without Congressional interference.

These are shameful counterweights to the humanitarian imperative of removing user fees. Whether the humanitarian claim prevails will depend, in significant part, on whether U.S. citizens act now to put an end to user fee nightmare.

Corporate Globalization
and the Poor

August 6, 2001

George Bush has thrown down the gauntlet, issuing a public challenge to the anti-corporate globalization movement. When hundreds of thousands last month demonstrated against the G-8 meeting of rich country leaders in Genoa, Italy, George Bush decried the activists, saying it was the advocates of corporate globalization who genuinely are seeking to advance the interests of the world's poor.

It's not enough to mock Bush's pretension of being a defender of the poor by pointing out that, through his giant tax cut, the president has overseen one of the history's great transfers of wealth to the rich in U.S. history. Critics must respond to his claims.

Unfortunately, that turns out to be a remarkably easy challenge to meet. The last 20 years of corporate globalization, even measured by the preferred indicators of the International Monetary Fund (IMF) and World Bank, have been a disaster for the world's poor.

Over the last two decades, Latin America has experienced stagnant growth, and African countries have seen incomes plummet. The only developing countries that have done well in the last two decades are those Asian countries that ignored the standard prescriptions of the IMF and World Bank.

The Washington, D.C.-based Center for Economic and Policy Research (CEPR) has published compelling data comparing growth rates from 1980 to 2000 (during the period of ascending IMF/World Bank power, when countries throughout the developing world adhered to the IMF/Bank structural adjustment policy package of slashing government spending, privatizating government-owned enterprises, liberalizing trade, orienting economies to exports and opening up countries to exploitative foreign investment) with the previous 20 year period (when many poor countries focused more on developing their own productive capacity and meeting local needs).

The results: "89 countries—77 percent, or more than three-fourths—saw their per capita rate of growth fall by at least five percentage points from the period (1960-1980) to the period (1980-2000). Only 14 countries—13 percent—saw their per capita rate of growth rise by that much from (1960-1980) to (1980-2000)."

CEPR found that the growth slowdown has been so severe that "18 countries—including several in Africa—would have more than twice as much income per person as they have today, if they had maintained the rate of growth in the last two decades that they had in the previous two decades. The average Mexican would have nearly twice as much income today, and the average Brazilian much more than twice as much, if not for the slowdown of economic growth over the last two decades."

A follow-up CEPR study used a similar methodology to look at social indicators. CEPR found that progress in reducing infant mortality, reducing child mortality, increasing literacy and increasing access to education has all slowed during the period of corporate globalization, especially in developing countries.

The CEPR global comparisons across time show the bottomline, combined effect of the specific policy components of corporate-friendly policies imposed by the IMF and World Bank and enforced by free trade agreements. These include the following:

- Trade Liberalization—The elimination of tariff protections for agriculture and industries in developing countries often leads to mass layoffs and displacement of the rural poor. In Mexico, for example, opening to U.S. agriculture imports has forced millions of poor farmers, who find themselves unable to compete with Cargill and Archer Daniels Midland, off the land.
- Privatization—IMF and World Bank structural adjust-

ment policies typically call for the sell off of government-owned enterprises to private owners, often foreign investors. Privatization is regularly associated with layoffs and pay cuts for workers in the privatized enterprises.

- Cuts in government spending—Reductions in government spending frequently reduce the ability of the government to provide services to the poor, exacerbating the social pain from rural displacement and industrial layoffs.
- Imposition of user fees—Many IMF and World Bank loans and programs call for the imposition of "user fees"—charges for the use of government-provided services like schools, health clinics and clean drinking water. For very poor people, even modest charges may result in the denial of access to services.
- Export promotion—Under structural adjustment programs, countries undertake a variety of measures to promote exports, at the expense of production for domestic needs. In the rural sector, the export orientation is often associated with the displacement of poor people who grow food for their own consumption, as their land is taken over by large plantations growing crops for foreign markets.
- Higher interest rates—Attractive to foreign investors, higher interest rates exert a recessionary effect on national economies, leading to higher rates of joblessness. Small businesses, often operated by women, find it more difficult to gain access to affordable credit, and often are unable to survive.

Advancing the interests of the poor has nothing to do with the corporate globalization agenda. This agenda is driven first by profit-seeking, and second by ideology.

But the corporate globalizers are nothing if not ambitious. They are seeking now to push fast-track negotiating authority through the U.S. Congress, to force all of Latin America into a NAFTA-style trade and investment agreement, launch a new World Trade Organization negotiating round, and intensify the IMF and World Bank's ability to impose structural adjustment through a sham debt relief process.

To lessen preventable human suffering, it is imperative that the protesters continue to build the movement against corporate globalization, with everything from street protests to citizen lobbying of Congress.

Another world is indeed possible, as the protesters are asserting. But for now the immediate challenge is to stop the corporate globalizers from making the existing one worse.

Thirsty for Justice

September 3, 2002

Shown the folly of over-reliance on markets even in the world's richest country, the market fundamentalists at the World Bank are continuing their push for privatization of services—with the provision of drinking water at the top of the list—in the developing world.

Water works plagued by poor service and underinvestment can be rejuvenated by private water operators. That according to the World Bank, a compromised consulting industry and the private water industry—dominated by the French firms Suez and Vivendi—itself.

But citizen movements across the planet are rising to challenge the World Bank and corporate schemes to wrest control of now-public water systems. Perhaps the hottest flashpoint in the conflict between the people and the Water Barons is in Ghana. There, the National Coalition Against the Privatization of Water (NCAP of Water) is aggressively opposing a Bank-advocated privatization scheme that would lease out the country's urban water systems for a song. The scheme was hatched in 1995, and may be implemented next year, unless NCAP can thwart it.

(A newly released International Fact-Finding Mission assessment of the Ghanaian privatization proposal is available at: http://www.citizen.org/documents/factfindingmission-Ghana.pdf)

To make the system generate enough revenue to pay the operator—a handful of international operators, including Suez and Vivendi, are in the running to take over the system—the privatization scheme would require persistent rate hikes. The goal is to achieve "cost recovery"—tariff revenue sufficient to meet operations and maintenance costs, without any public subsidy to keep prices in check. This, even though systems in the United States, among other industrialized countries, routinely rely on support from general tax revenues.

Compounding the rate hikes, the privatization scheme calls for the inclusion of an "automatic tariff adjustment"—with rates rising automatically to offset inflation and, most importantly, currency devaluations. That makes sense from the viewpoint of the foreign operator—they will want to maintain constant profits in dollar-denominated terms, not in cedis, the local currency. But it is a disaster from the point of view of Ghanaian consumers—their cedi income does not go up just because the value of the cedi declines. Assuming future devaluations, Ghanaian consumers will find themselves paying a higher and higher proportion of their income to the water company.

In exchange for certain, ongoing rate hikes into the indefinite future, Ghana is supposed to benefit from a more reliable and efficient system, and from expansion of the piped water system to reach the millions of urban consumers who are not connected to water pipes. But almost all of the evidence suggests these promises will turn out to be illusions or deceptions.

First, the record of private water company operation in developing countries is very poor. There is little to suggest that private companies deliver "efficiencies" in this area, though they are clearly skilled at extracting enormous profits.

The details of the Ghanaian privatization plans offer little comfort that things will be different in this case.

There are some incentives built in the proposal to increase the amount of water delivered—many lower income Ghanaians may get water from pipes only once every two or four weeks— but the proposed leasing terms would encourage the private operator to improve service for high-volume richer consumers, rather than low-volume poorer ones.

Achievement of water delivery and other performance standards would be self-monitored by the private water operator, overseen by a newly created regulatory agency with little experience and little chance of effectively controlling a giant multinational.

The proposed leasing arrangements impose only the most minimal investment requirements on the private operator (who would lease the system, rather than purchase it outright)—and the operator is guaranteed a return even on that minimal investment, making it more of a loan than actual investment. So the operator will offer almost nothing in terms of new money for repairs or pipe expansion.

There is some new money promised in the deal for pipe expansion. But the money will all be in the form of new loans and some grants from the World Bank and donor countries. The private operator does nothing to obtain these loans, and has no pay-back obligations. This money—desperately needed for system expansion—could be made available right now (or could have been provided five years earlier), but the Bank and donors have made the loans and grants conditional on privatization.

Even this money is far less than needed to connect most urban Ghanaians to the piped water system. They will continue to rely on exploitative private water tanker operators, who buy water in bulk from the water utility, drive to areas without piped water service and sell to consumers at rates five or ten times that of price of piped water. The poorest people in cities have no choice but to rely on these water sources, and find themselves spending 10, 15 or even 20 percent of their income on drinking water.

The tanker prices could easily be controlled. The utility could operate tankers and sell tanker-provided water at the piped water rate. Or the private tankers could be tolerated, but required to sell water at a regulated price—with the utility refusing to sell water to those tanker operators who fail to comply.

The World Bank has not considered these approaches, and at least one pro-privatization consultant's document suggests that such measures would interfere with the flourishing private market in water provision!

NCAP of Water, like colleagues around Africa and else-

where in the developing world, rejects this market fundamentalist illogic. They insist that drinking water be treated as a
right, not a commodity. Rather than inviting predatory multinationals in to drive up prices, suck up profits, serve the urban
elite, and ignore the poor, they say, the public sector can and
must be reinvigorated to ensure decent delivery of water, one of
life's essentials.

Of Caviar and Capitalism

December 17, 2002

Are capitalism and caviar incompatible? Is the system that prides itself on the creation and veneration of wealth unable to maintain a sustainable market for one of the great trappings of wealth?

Well, at the very least, the tragic story of the global caviar industry gives pause. It stands as a parable illustrating the pitfalls of the market fundamentalist ideology that has dominated global economic policy-making for two decades.

The story of the industry is recounted in a new book by Inga Saffron, a Philadelphia Inquirer reporter and former Moscow correspondent for the paper, Caviar: The Strange History and Uncertain Future of the World's Most Coveted Delicacy (New York: Broadway Books).

For most of the twentieth century, the world caviar market was supplied primarily by the Soviet Union. Caviar—the salted eggs of sturgeon or paddlefish—is a creation of Russian culture. Although sturgeon once populated many of the world's great seas and rivers in large numbers, most of the world's supply after World War I came from the Caspian Sea and the Black Sea.

After coming to power, Saffron says, "the Soviets realized they could make a lot of money if they controlled the caviar market."

They exported the product to Western markets to earn hard currency, but limited supply to increase prices.

"I don't want to say that they had a great environmental record, because they didn't," Saffron says. "But they did act as a brake on fishing because they limited caviar exports."

Even when the Soviets embarked on their disastrous dam-building schemes, which blocked sturgeon from swimming upstream to spawn, they developed an extensive hatchery system that maintained the sturgeon population.

Communism, it turned out, was pretty good for caviar.

When the Soviet Union collapsed, so did the protections and support system for caviar.

In the chaos following the fall of the Soviet Union, factories across the country stopped doing business as government money for operating expenses evaporated. Funding to maintain the hatcheries similarly disappeared, and the hatchery system fell apart. Overall, Saffron says, the hatchery system became much less efficient, and was able to put back many fewer fish than it had before.

Even worse, perhaps, was the rampant poaching that occurred after the fall of the USSR.

"Many of the people who had been thrown out of work began to fish illegally," according to Saffron. "They began to poach for sturgeon and make caviar in their kitchens, because that is the only way they could make money. It was the one resource in Southern Russia."

The old Soviet limits on fishing "were ignored, and people just fished all the time," she says.

Enforcement agencies were weak and ineffectual. Many were bought off or intimidated by the criminal gangs that gained control over much of the industry.

Today, the sturgeon in the Russian and Kazakhstan portions of the Caspian are in steep decline, and Saffron has little hope that they will be saved. International controls on caviar imports are coming too little, too late, and in any case cannot stop the internal traffic in the delicacy.

The collapse of the sturgeon in the Russian and Kazakhstan portions of the Caspian is history repeating itself. Rampant overfishing led to the rapid destruction of sturgeon populations in Germany, France, the Eastern United States and the U.S. Great Lakes, all in a matter of decades in the late nineteenth and early twentieth centuries.

Today, the counterexample to the laissez-faire caviar failure is Iran. Like the Soviet Union once did, Iran maintains strong limits on fish catch in its portion of the Caspian and operates a sophisticated and effective hatchery system.

Countries relying only on price signals to regulate the industry have witnessed a short cycle of boom and bust.

Countries that have succeeded in maintaining a viable caviar industry over time have made long-term investments in infrastructure and put in place systems to ensure sustainable management of limited resources.

Those are key elements for effective economic management and a livable world.

Markets alone will not deliver them.

We Had a Democracy Once, But You Crushed It

August 8, 2003

In yesterday's *Washington Post*, Condoleeza Rice, the President's National Security Advisor, writes the following:

"Our task is to work with those in the Middle East who seek progress toward greater democracy, tolerance, prosperity and freedom. As President Bush said in February, 'The world has a clear interest in the spread of democratic values, because stable and free nations do not breed ideologies of murder. They encourage the peaceful pursuit of a better life.'"

Now, if we only had a nickel for every time Bush, or Rice, or Colin Powell, or Paul Wolfowitz or Dick Cheney or Richard Perle or Donald Rumsfeld talked about bringing democracy to the Middle East.

Talk, talk, talk.

Here's something you can bet on: Rumsfeld and Wolfowitz will not hold a press conference this month to commemorate the 50th anniversary of the U.S.-led coup of the democratically elected leader of Iran—Mohammed Mossadegh.

Rice and Powell won't hold a press conference to celebrate Operation Ajax, the CIA plot that overthrew the Mossadegh.

That was 50 years ago this month, in August 1953.

That's when Mossadegh was fed up with the Anglo-Iranian Oil Company—now BP—pumping Iran's oil and shipping the profits back home to the United Kingdom.

And Mossadegh said—hey, this is our oil, I think we'll keep it.

And Winston Churchill said—no you won't.

Mossadegh nationalized the company—the way the British were nationalizing their own vital industries at the time.

But what's good for the UK ain't good for Iran.

If you fly out of Dulles Airport in Virginia, ever wonder what the word Dulles means?

It stands for the Dulles family—Secretary of State John Foster Dulles and his brother, the CIA director, Allen Dulles.

They were responsible for the overthrow of the democratically elected leader of Iran.

As was President Theodore Roosevelt's grandson, Kermit Roosevelt, the CIA agent who traveled to Iran to pull off the coup.

Now why should we be concerned about a coup that happened so far away almost 50 years ago this month?

New York Times reporter Stephen Kinzer puts it this way:

"It is not far-fetched to draw a line from Operation Ajax through the Shah's repressive regime and the Islamic revolution to the fireballs that engulfed the World Trade Center in New York."

Kinzer has written a remarkable new book, *All the Shah's Men: An American Coup and the Roots of Middle East Terror* (Wiley, 2003).

In it, he documents step by step, how Roosevelt, the Dulles boys and Norman Schwarzkopf Sr., among a host of others, took down a democratically elected regime in Iran.

They had freedom of the press. We shut it down.

They had democracy. And we crushed it.

Mossadegh was the beacon of hope for the Middle East.

If democracy were allowed to take hold in Iran, it probably would have spread throughout the Middle East.

We asked Kinzer—what does the overthrow of Mossadegh say about the United States respect for democracy abroad?

"Imagine today what it must sound like to Iranians to hear American leaders tell them, 'We want you to have a democracy in Iran, we disapprove of your present government, we wish to help you bring democracy to your country.' Naturally, they roll their eyes and say—"We had a democracy once, but you crushed it,'" he said. "This shows how differently other people perceive us from the way we perceive ourselves. We think of ourselves as paladins of democracy. But actually, in Iran, we destroyed the last democratic regime the country ever had and set them on a road to what has been half a century of dictatorship."

After ousting Mossadegh, the United States put in place a brutal Shah who destroyed dissent and tortured the dissenters.

And the Shah begat the Islamic revolution.

During that Islamic revolution in 1979, Iranians held up Mossadegh's picture, telling the world—we want a democratic regime that resists foreign influence and respects the will of the Iranian people as expressed through democratic institutions.

"They were never able to achieve that. And this has led many Iranians to react very poignantly to my book," Kaizer told us. "One woman sent me an e-mail that said, 'I was in tears when I finished your book because it made me think of all we lost and all we could have had.'"

Of course, the overthrow of Mossadegh was only one of the first U.S. coups of a democratically elected regime. (To see one in movie form, pick up a copy of Raoul Peck's Lumumba, now on DVD.)

Kinzer's previous books include *Bitter Fruit: The Story of the American Coup in Guatemala.*

He's thinking of putting together a boxed set of his books on American coups.

Get copies of *Bitter Fruit* and *All The Shah's Men.*

Read them.

And the next time a politician talks about spreading democracy around the globe, ask them about Mohammed Mossadegh in Iran, Patrice Lumumba in the Congo, and Jacobo Arbenz in Guatemala.

Corporations and Their Proxies Defeated in Miami—But They Refuse to Give Up

November 25, 2003

There was good news and bad news from inside the negotiations of the Ministerial meeting for the Free Trade Area of the Americas (FTAA), held last week in Miami.

The good news: Brazil has succeeded in putting forward a framework that would alleviate the worst aspects of the U.S.-backed extremist proposals that threaten public health, the environment, and worker rights. With mobilized populations at home demanding nothing less, Brazil, Argentina and other countries appear to have defeated the U.S. effort to expand NAFTA to the entire hemisphere.

In at least four separate places, the final statement of the meeting, known as the Ministerial Declaration, reiterates the need for a "balanced" agreement. The key phrase of the Declaration states that, "Ministers recognize that countries may assume different levels of commitments."

What this means in practice is that countries will not be required to adhere to the market fundamentalist proposals advanced by the United States in the areas of intellectual property, investment, services and other areas.

While it would be best if there were no agreements in these areas whatsoever—since the agreements in various ways are designed to subordinate public interest considerations to the commercial interests of multinational corporations—at least no country will be required to agree to these proposals as a condition of participating in the FTAA.

Those countries that agree to specific commitments, in the investment area, say, will be required to honor them. But none of the Latin American or Caribbean countries have any real interest in doing so. There aren't many Uruguayan or Honduran investors looking for special protections in the U.S. market.

Brazil gained the upper hand by responding effectively to the U.S. position that it could not negotiate key agricultural issues within the FTAA. U.S. negotiators said they wanted to move on agricultural issues of concern to Brazil and other countries, but these matters had to be handled at the World Trade Organization (WTO), where they could be negotiated as well with the European Union and Japan. Well, said Brazil, if agriculture is a WTO issue, then so is intellectual property, which is already covered by a WTO agreement, and so are other controversial issues.

Given this move by Brazil, the United States was happy to maintain even opt-in agreements as part of the FTAA.

But there's no question the United States has lost its ability to impose its maniacal NAFTA vision on the hemisphere. "This is not what we wanted, and we have serious concerns," said Frank Vargo, U.S. National Association of Manufacturers vice president for international economic affairs. A good sign.

Unfortunately, the inside news from Miami wasn't all good. The United States violated the spirit of the ministerial declaration by announcing an intensified strategy of negotiating bilateral and mini-regional agreements containing exactly the horrific proposals—on intellectual property, investment, and other areas—that it failed to ram through in the FTAA.

The United States has already concluded a free trade agreement with Chile, and is scheduled to conclude negotiations over a free trade agreement with the Central American countries next month. In Miami, U.S. Trade Representative Robert Zoellick announced that the United States would soon commence negotiations over trade deals with the Dominican Republic, Panama, Colombia and Peru, as well as supposedly with Ecuador and Bolivia.

We asked the trade minister of a small country, the Bahamas, what he thought about the U.S. strategy of negotiating bilaterals.

"Most countries in the hemisphere have concerns" about the U.S. approach, Bahamian Minister of Trade and Industry Leslie Miller told us. "It's just pressure tactics. The U.S. wants to consolidate its position."

The strategy is euphemistically called "competitive liberalization" by its advocates, but it's little more than divide and conquer. The idea is to pit countries in the hemisphere against each other, negotiating individual deals that offer incremental benefits of improved access to the U.S. market, in exchange for massive concessions for U.S. multinationals. As countries watch others enter into free trade deals, they worry about being left behind, and agree to similar terms.

Whereas developing countries when united can stand up to U.S. pressure and demands, in isolation and in competition with each other, they are easy pickings.

Notwithstanding the benefits, this strategy has significant limitations from the U.S. corporate perspective, which is why some business groups have been publicly critical. The strategy requires too many negotiations with too many countries, and may leave the biggest markets out. Noting that Chile and Mexico already have free trade deals with the United States, Mark Weisbrot of the Washington, D.C.-based Center for Economic and Policy Research points out that 70 percent of the remaining Latin American market (measured by economic output) is attributable to Brazil, Argentina and Venezuela—countries with no interest in signing on to bilateral agreements with the United States that advance the U.S. extremist economic agenda.

Still, there's no getting around the fact that existing trade pacts, plus those under negotiation and those for which negotiations are pending, will lock up a huge chunk of Latin America, and significantly deprive countries of freedom to pursue independent economic policies.

Whether the USTR bilateral trade agreement offensive can be halted may turn on the U.S.-Central American agreement. If brought before the U.S. Congress next year and defeated, U.S. trade negotiators may be forced to abandon their present approach. A victory for U.S. negotiators and their business controllers will give renewed life to a model that has failed by any objective measure, other than serving multinational corporate interests.

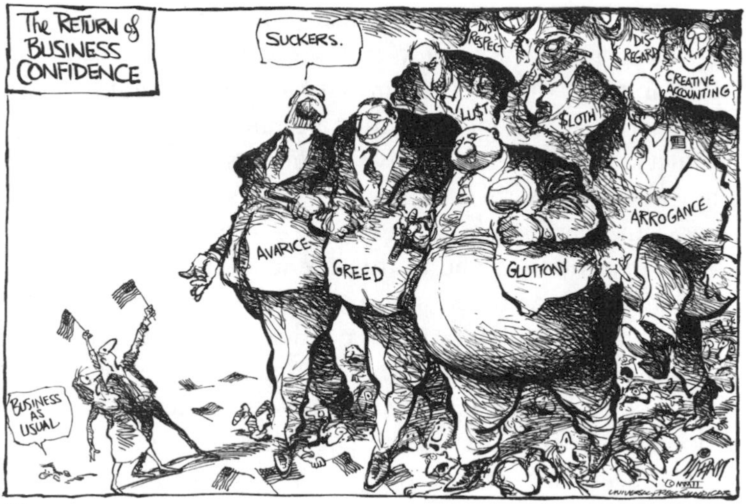

PART FOUR

THE CORPORATIST OCTOPUS

Rampant commercialism—so excessive now that it is difficult to parody—degrades our public space and displaces noncommercial values such as cooperation, community, altruism. And, in ways we do not realize, it constricts our sense of the politically possible and the politically unpalatable.

Corporations routinely sponsor community events and community institutions—from softball tournaments to chili cook-offs, from schools to public beaches—to advertise their products, including to captive audiences of schoolchildren. They also seek by their sponsorships to gain a reputation as a responsible member of the community—it is important for their political positioning that, to the extent possible, people see the companies as "one of us," not an intrusive outsider. Thus, one outgrowth of the colonization of public space is the colonization of our minds. Ways of arranging life that do not involve corporations or do not serve corporate interests—whether in the traditional economy, provision of public services, entertainment; or via demands for lessening economic inequality, within nations and across borders—become harder and harder to conceptualize.

Since corporations have positioned themselves as part of the community, it seems natural for them to claim the same rights—like free speech—as human beings. We need to continually remind ourselves that corporations are, in fact, different. Unfortunately, the academy, which might be a source of critical reflection on corporate encroachment on politics and public space, appears significantly oblivious to the phenomenon. And while the corporate media sometimes do a decent job of uncovering particular business abuses (though more often they do not), they almost never challenge fundamental corporate prerogatives.

City for Sale

February 15, 1999

It used to be easy to mock the excesses of commercialism through parody that revealed the cost of commercial appropriation of public and community space.

No more, thanks to Sacramento, California's state capital.

Last year, the Sacramento City Council approved a plan to launch a "Capital Spirit" corporate sponsorship program that will blanket the city. The program is just now getting under way, with sponsorship deals for non-alcoholic beverage and telecommunications companies under negotiation.

A feasibility study prepared by The Wilkinson Group, a consulting firm hired by the city, recommends a wide-ranging corporate sponsorship program involving all city departments. When the program is fully operational, the consulting firm projects an earning stream for the city of $2 million to $5 million a year.

The city's plan calls for: an official car rental partner for the city (potential partners named include Avis, Budget, Enterprise and Thrifty), a preferred ice cream (potential partners: Baskin Robbins, Dreyers, Nestle), preferred food suppliers for the police and fire departments and the convention center, an official film (potential partners: Fuji, Kodak, Polaroid), an official delivery service (potential partners: Airborne Express, DHL, U.S. Postal Service, FedEx, UPS), a preferred coffee and an official departmental coffee supplier (potential partners: Java Centrale, Maxwell House, Folger's, Millstone, Pete's, Starbucks), official wear for park and recreation staff (potential partners include REI), official software and official computer of Sacramento, official computer of specific departments (potential partners include: Oracle, Sun, Apple, 3COM), exclusive security for Sacramento, and more.

Our favorite: official undergarment supplier for city police, fire and security!

From the city's point of view, these are opportunities too good to pass up. Using "existing facilities," at no cost to the city, explains Sacramento Senior Management Analyst Michelle Nelson, Sacramento will generate funds to improve parks and recreational facilities, and to undertake other capital improvements.

The potential income stream will be, at most, little more than 1 percent of Sacramento's $451 million annual budget, but Nelson says the money will be used for investments that would otherwise not be funded. California law makes it difficult or impossible for cities to act to raise their own taxes.

There is no illusion in the Sacramento program that the corporate contributions are charity—this is not a low-key adopt-a-highway-style program. Instead, explains the consultant report, "When establishing a sponsorship program, a property must clearly indicate how sponsorship of their program will positively impact the sponsor's revenue streams."

Key elements in delivering value to sponsors include: giving sponsors the imprimatur of official city approval, providing sponsors with exclusive marketing rights in designated areas (zoos, parks, historic tourist areas, etc), enabling the companies to seem "part of the community" (by identifying a refurbished teen center, for example, as "paid for by The Gap") and providing "signage" on public properties in highly trafficked areas.

Yet all of these ways of "providing specific business development opportunities and marketing-based benefits to prospective sponsors," as The Wilkinson Group calls them, are, individually and collectively, deeply troubling.

Selling the city's de facto stamp of approval will inevitably place the city in the position of endorsing corporate polluters, labor-rights-violators, criminals and wrongdoers, as well as unhealthy or harmful products, such as sugar-filled soda. In some cases, the de facto stamp of approval would be an actual city endorsement. For health plans, the consultant plan suggests offering sponsors a "City of Sacramento testimonial to health care provision."

The exclusive marketing rights offers outrageously facilitate consumer rip-offs and denial of choice. If they are thirsty, why should people strolling through the zoo be limited to Coke products in their product selection? Why should they be made to pay premium prices? In a very real way, the sale of exclusive marketing rights camouflages a hidden tax on consumers in the cloak of corporate generosity.

The sale of "signage"—indeed, the entire program—marks a further encroachment of commercial values into public space and the public realm. There is a proper line delineating the public from the corporate, and government from business. The spheres represent different values, operate according to different motivations and serve different purposes. But when the commercial and public spheres overlap, it is the corporate sphere that blots out the public, never the reverse.

To this, the city council's response is, according to Michelle Nelson: "Trust us." The sponsorships will be tasteful, balanced and not harm "what we hold valuable."

Well, maybe they still do have a sense of humor in Sacramento.

Ralph Reed Meets
Jim Metrock

May 30, 1999

Alabama Senator Richard Shelby could safely be described as a pro-business Republican.

But if nothing else, Shelby believes in constituent service, and one of his constituents is Jim Metrock, another pro-business Alabaman who tends to vote Republican.

As CEO of Metrock Wire and Steel, a family business, and founder of the Business Council of Alabama, the state's largest business association, Jim Metrock had dealings with Senator Shelby. A couple of years ago, Metrock decided to get out of the steel business and do some community service.

Metrock was concerned with commercial television's assault on children.

After Pat Ellis, a fellow Alabaman, told Metrock about Channel One, he began to research the problem. Metrock was surprised by what he learned—a marketing company was assaulting eight million children across the country with ads for junk food among other items.

Channel One Network, now owned by Primedia, Inc., is the company that loans televisions to public schools, in exchange for the schools agreeing to give Channel One access to schoolchildren for 12 minutes every day. The marketers use this opportunity to pump the children with a 10 minute "news" program, generally aired during home room, and two minutes of commercials pushing such nutritious staples as Pepsi, Mountain Dew, Snickers, M&M's, Twix, Bubble Yum bubble gum, Extra bubble gum and Fruit Loops, among other consumer items.

The advertisers pay a hefty price for the ads, a reported $200,000 for a 30-second spot.

Metrock asked his 18-year-old son if he had ever heard of Channel One.

Yes, the son said, I've been watching it for three years.

Flabbergasted, Metrock launched his campaign. Early last year, Metrock and Ellis traveled to Washington, D.C. to meet with Senator Shelby's staff about the problem. In April 1998, Senator Shelby issued a news release expressing his concerns about Channel One and calling for Congressional hearings.

Channel One was not pleased. Executives pulled out their checkbooks and began writing $120,000 worth of checks to lobbyists in an effort to derail the hearings.

First, they put on retainer an inside-the-beltway power law firm—Preston, Gates. Then they brought on Ralph Reed, the former executive director of the Christian Coalition turned corporate lobbyist. And then they hired a lobbyist in Alabama to keep an eye on things.

Well, the months rolled by, and the lobbyists lobbied, and the hearing date was delayed and delayed and delayed. Until this spring, when the hearing was set in stone for May 20, 1999.

Then, all of the sudden, radio spots started airing in Alabama attacking Senator Shelby, implying that he was part of a left-wing plot to put the kibosh on the pro-Christian values of Channel One. We kid you not.

Here is the text of one of the ads that ran:

"Tragedies like Littleton, Colorado show how vital it is to teach our children the values of faith and family. One bright spot is Channel One. Channel One reaches 8 million students every school day, 250,000 here in Alabama, with a television program that tells children to turn their backs on drugs, reject violence and abstain from sex before marriage. And it's working. The Partnership for a Drug-Free America found that children are more aware of the risks of using marijuana because they are watching Channel One. But some on the radical left want Congress to ban such programming. Call Senator Shelby ... and tell him to stand up for Channel One's right to teach our kids to say 'no' to drugs and 'no' to sex before marriage. ..."

The ad was sponsored by an unknown group called the Coalition to Protect Our Children. The group has a

Montgomery, Alabama post office box. But it has no listed phone number. And Metrock says he knows of no organization in Alabama that endorses Channel One.

Channel One's lobbyist in Alabama is a man named Martin Christie. Metrock spoke with Christie on May 17 and Christie told him that he knew nothing about the campaign against Senator Shelby.

"I asked Ralph Reed if he knew anything about this advertising campaign in Alabama," Metrock says. "He didn't say he didn't. He said that he just wasn't keeping up with that."

He asked a Channel One executive if the company had anything to do with the ad, and the executive said no.

In any event, the campaign to derail the hearing failed. It was held on May 20. Ralph Nader and Phyllis Schlafly spoke against Channel One, while a Channel One executive and a priest from a religious school in Washington, D.C. spoke in favor of Channel One. The hearing gained very little press attention—an article in the Birmingham News, a spot on National Public Radio's Morning Edition.

But the hearing has reinvigorated Metrock's determination to defeat commercialism in the schools. He wants to start with Channel One in home rooms—which he calls "a two-by-four to the head"—and then proceed on to Coke and Pepsi in the hallways.

Toast

About six years ago, a friend gave us a toaster. It was a present. The friend bought the toaster from Williams-Sonoma, the San Francisco-based kitchen store, with outlets in upscale malls throughout the United States. It was a modern toaster, which means first, that it was made primarily out of plastic instead of stainless steel, second, it had all kinds of gizmos on it, and third, if something goes wrong with it, in all likelihood, because of the modern electronic devices embedded in it, you won't be able to fix it.

On these new modern toasters, you can calibrate the shade of the toast—you can set the toaster for lighter or darker toast.

Our first plastic toaster lasted about two years before it stopped toasting.

Luckily, Williams-Sonoma will replace any item if you are "not satisfied with your purchase for any reason."

We took it back to the store here in Washington, D.C. and told the sales clerk that we received the toaster as a present purchased from Williams-Sonoma and that the toaster wasn't working. The sales clerk said—no problem, here's a new one.

And she handed over a brand new Kenwood Four Slice plastic toaster, which lasted a little longer than a year, before it stopped toasting. So, we took the Kenwood back and told the clerk at the store what happened and the clerk said—no problem, and she handed over a new toaster—different make, this one was a Toastronic Ultra.

The following year, same problem. And same solution. We turned in the Toastronic Ultra and return it for a Kitchen Aid Toaster.

Last week, the Kitchen Aid Toaster stopped toasting on one side. We took it in to the Williams-Sonoma, and the clerk handed over a Cuisinart plastic toaster.

The Cuisinart toaster has all kinds of features, including a

Bagel button, a defrost button, a reheat button, the now traditional lighter and darker buttons, a cancel reset button, and
most annoyingly, a "shade control" panel, which in bright red
lights (just what you don't want to see in the morning) tells you
where exactly on a scale of very light toast to very dark toast you
have calibrated your new toaster for this morning.

We have a friend who is a super cautious person, but who
believes that toasters should last a lifetime. (Forgive him—he is
from a different era.) So anyway, he gets one of these new plastic toasters, and the plastic lever falls off. Now everytime he
wants toast, he throws caution to the wind and sticks a butter
knife into the toaster's lever slot to hold down the lever until it
clicks in.

Annoyed at this repeated failure of modern technology, we
called Williams-Sonoma's customer service line. The sales person answered and we told her our story about returning the plastic toasters periodically to her store. She said she didn't think
she could do anything about the complaint. We asked—why
not just sell a toaster that lasts? And she said—we do. It's stainless steel Dualit Combi Toaster and it sells for $319.00. The
plastic Cuisinart that we just received sells for $99.95.

"You can buy the Dualit and it will toast for you well into
your 90s," she said with a snicker.

In San Francisco, Williams-Sonoma spokesperson Tracy
Brown told us that her store tries to sell the "newest and greatest" products. She said she checked with a buyer, and com-
plaints about toasters breaking down "are not common."

Brown then called back to report that "we identified reli-
ability problems with the Kitchen Aid and that's why we got rid
of it."

"We really believe that the Cuisinart toaster will last," she
said.

Now, of course, we remember our parents' toasters—the
aluminum Toastmasters that they toasted with—toasters that
lasted a lifetime. These classic toasters had no bagel button, no

defrost button, no reheat button, and definitely no shade control panel.

You simply stuck the slices of bread into the slot, pushed down the lever, and waited for the toast to pop up.

So, with all the wonders of modern technology, why can't the companies make a reasonably priced toaster that lasts?

We put this question to Holly Smith-Berry, marketing director at the Columbia, Missouri based Toastmaster, the company that sold the first pop up toaster in 1926 (Model 1A-1) for $12.50.

"We get letters from our customers, wanting to send us their old Toastmaster toasters, telling us they love the triple loop design on the side of the toaster, and they are amazed at how long they have lasted—50 or 60 years, in some cases," Smith-Berry said. "But if you took our 1940 steel toaster and costed it out for inflation, it would cost $170 today."

She said that Toastmaster toasters today range from $10 to $30 and they are tested to last for 12 or so years.

"We've seen toasters selling in Wal-Mart for $7.96," she said. "So, if you don't want to clean the crumbs out of your toaster, you can just get rid of it and buy a new one."

"Unfortunately, we live in a more disposable society," she says.

Toastmaster makes a heavy duty toaster, but it's built in Germany by Bosch Siemens, it's designed by Porsche, and it sells for $225.

The decline of the reliable, reasonably priced toaster is symbolic of what's gone wrong with modern society—shoddy products, disposable society, planned obsolescence, high-tech but no respect.

Shade control in, quality out.

A Not So Academic Oversight

September 19, 2000

The American Political Science Association's annual convention recently came through town, filling up Washington, D.C. hotels with thousands of academics ready to present their latest research findings.

Browsing through the convention's program, we hoped to learn of new findings on the role of corporations in the political process. Instead, we found that there appeared to be virtually no papers on or even referencing corporate power.

That's a little strange, we thought. After all, it is hardly a controversial claim these days that corporations exert a major if not decisive influence over politics, in the United States and around the world.

We decided to make sure our impression that corporations were absent from the convention papers was correct. The American Political Science Association has conveniently posted on its website approximately a thousand of the papers presented at the conference, and the site has a good search engine.

We searched through these thousand abstracts for the word "corporation." Two hits.

We tried again, this time using the word "corporate." This time we came up with 11 hits. We did another search, for the word "business." After eliminating abstracts that use the word "business" in a context where it means something other than corporations (i.e., a reference to Congressional business), we wound up with 23 hits.

In total, three dozen abstracts even mention the words "corporation," "corporate," or "business"—3.6 percent of the roughly thousand abstracts we searched. This is only a rough approximation of the number that actually discuss corporate power. The vast majority of those we found refer to corporations, but don't have corporate power as their focus. On the other hand, our search undoubtedly missed some papers that implicitly discuss corporate power—say, with a focus on labor relations—but don't use any of our key words.

Disturbed by the results of this survey, we asked some of those who had presented papers that discuss corporations to ruminate on our findings.

Scott Pegg, an assistant professor in the Department of International Relations at Bilkent University, in Ankara, Turkey, shared some particularly interesting reactions. (Pegg's paper topic: "Corporate Armies for States and State Armies for Corporations: Addressing the Challenges of Globalization and Natural Resource Conflict.")

First, he validated our sense that the findings of our survey constituted a remarkable oversight. "The three largest subfields of [U.S.] political science are American government/politics, comparative politics and international relations. The study of transnational corporations is relevant to all three of them," Pegg says. "In particular, in an election year, I find it stunning that the huge numbers of people working on the American electoral system and presidential politics would be neglecting the corporate role in bankrolling politicians to such a degree." Our sentiments exactly.

Asked to account for the corporate studies vacuum, Pegg suggests several explanations. Corporations may fall through disciplinary cracks, he says—they aren't the traditional political actors on which political scientists focus. Corporations are reluctant to share information that academics need to conduct their research, he points out, and information that is available tends to come from nongovernmental organizations with which many academics are not familiar. Academics tend to reward theoretical inquiries over empirical investigations. And, he says, "many academics are interested in securing outside funding for their research projects. Corporate funding is available for some projects, but probably not for those that critically assess corporate crimes or corporate human rights violations."

To check that the results of our survey were not a fluke, we did a similar search on all U.S. dissertations published in the last two years. The results were similar. After we eliminated those that mentioned corporations in completely irrelevant contexts (e.g., thanking a nonprofit funder with corporation in its name, or mentioning that a corporation had invented a scientific process used in the dissertation) we found 75 dissertations that included the word "corporation" in their abstract. As a point of comparison, 43 dissertations used the word "baseball" in their abstract, and 1,008 included the word "war."

We can't help but draw depressing conclusions from our surveys.

One of the sources of corporate power is that corporations appear both everywhere and nowhere at the same time. With the commercialism explosion of recent years, there are fewer and fewer public spaces free from corporate logos. At the same time, the dominant political and social culture orients us away from assessing the many ways that corporations shape the contours of our politics, life opportunities, even our leisure time.

We would hope that the academy might be a place where researchers would seek to break through corporate hegemony, and undertake empirical and theoretical investigations of the manifestations and consequences of concentrated corporate power.

Of course, these hopes may someday be realized. If protests challenging corporate power continue their recent upsurge, academic inquiry will, eventually, follow.

But for intellectual leadership, it appears we should look to the undergraduates in the streets, not the professoriate.

The Real Thing:
Democracy as a Contact Sport

December 13, 2000

A couple weeks ago, we received an invitation to attend an event at the Library of Congress.

Coca-Cola was about to make an "historic contribution" to the Library of Congress, and the Library, and Coca-Cola, were inviting reporters to cover the event. We accepted the invitation.

We learned from the morning papers that the "historic contribution" was a complete set of 20,000 television commercials pushing Coca-Cola into the American digestive system. Remember the one where the kid hands Pittsburgh Steeler Mean Joe Greene his bottle of Coke, and in return, Mean Joe tosses the kid his football jersey? Or what about on a hilltop in Italy where the folks start sing "I'd like to buy the world a Coke and keep it company"?

The event was at the Great Hall of the Thomas Jefferson Building—named after the Thomas Jefferson who, in 1816, wrote: "I hope we shall crush in its birth the aristocracy of our monied corporations which dare already to challenge our government to a trial of strength, and bid defiance to the laws our country."

Anyway, we pull up at the appointed hour (7:15 p.m. on November 29, 2000) at the Thomas Jefferson building, and there's a traffic jam created by stretch limousines blocking the entrance.

In addition to lowly reporters, the 400 or so guests included ambassadors, members of Congress, corporate chieftains and other dignitaries. Good thing we dressed up.

The Main Hall is this absolutely stunning room, with marble staircases. A string quartet is playing. Waiters are serving Coke in classic bottles. The food is fabulous—lamb chops, trout, Peking duck. We rub shoulders with the Ambassador from Burma.

The "aristocracy of our monied corporations," as Jefferson put it, had taken over the place, and Coca-Cola wanted to make sure that everybody knew it.

After all, Coke could have just donated the ads to the Library and left it at that. But this wasn't about Coke's largesse. It was about public relations—whether the public would view the company as a racist company (Coke had just agreed to pay $192.5 million to settle allegations that it routinely discriminated against black employees in pay, promotions and performance evaluations) or a junk food pusher (consuming large quantities of sugared Coca-Cola has led to ours being one of the most overweight generations in history)—or instead, a generous contributor to the Library of Congress.

James Billington, the Librarian of Congress, was called on to deliver good things to Coke, and he did. He turned over the keys of the Main Hall to Coke, and Coke decked the place out with its logo, stitched in red beside the logo of the Library of Congress. Television sets were placed throughout the hall, the better for the Ambassadors and members of the Democratic Leadership Council to check out the commercials.

Billington was selling the soul of the library to one of the world's most powerful corporations. In addition to the ads, Coke was establishing a fellowship at the Library for the study of "culture and communication"—one fellow will receive $20,000 a year for the next five years.

Gary Ruskin, director of Commercial Alert, was outside the event, protesting. "It is not the proper role of the taxpayer-financed Library of Congress to help promote junk food like Coca-Cola to a nation that is suffering skyrocketing levels of obesity," Ruskin said. "It is crass commercialism for James Billington to degrade Jefferson's library and founding ideals into a huckster's backdrop."

But without shame, Billington introduced Doug Daft, the president of Coca-Cola, who said that "Coca-Cola has become an integral part of people's lives by helping to tell these stories."

Nothing about profits. Nothing about overweight kids. Nothing about racism.

After Daft spoke, the room went dark, and the ads ran on the television screens. Nostalgia swept the room. When the ads were finished, the lights went back on and the crowd cheered.

About 80 high school students, dressed in Coca-Cola red sweaters, filled the marble staircases and sang—"I want to buy the world a Coke." Again, the crowd cheered. Doug Daft, standing downstairs, came back to the microphone to continue his statement. We were upstairs at this point, and we looked down at him and asked, in a loud voice—"Why are you using a public library to promote a junk food product?"

The room went quiet. Library of Congress police charged up the marble staircase. Doug Daft put his hand to his ear and shouted back to us: "What did you say?"

In a louder voice, we shouted back: "Why are you using a public institution to promote a junk food product?"

The next thing we know, we are on the ground. The Library of Congress police had tackled us. Again, the crowd cheered—not for our question, but for the tackle.

We were dragged downstairs, past the Ambassador from Burma, and hauled outside, where police officers from the District of Columbia were waiting for us.

Out of the Thomas Jefferson building came running a man from Coke. "This is a private event," the man from Coke told the police. "I'm from Coca-Cola."

At first, the police wanted nothing to do with the man from Coke. But the man from Coke insisted. They huddled.

Apparently, the man from Coke didn't want us arrested for asking an obvious question. Apparently, the man from Coke didn't want a public trial. The man from Coke was standing up for our First Amendment rights to ask his boss a question.

The police said we were to leave the grounds. And we weren't to come back. Ever.

Blue Light Special at the Smithsonian

February 17, 2001

Lawrence Small has a great corporate pedigree.

For 27 years, Small was a top executive with Citicorp/Citibank. In 1991, he became president of Fannie Mae, the bully on the housing finance market.

Last year, he became Secretary of the Smithsonian Institution. He didn't bother resigning from the many corporate boards on which he sits today, including The Chubb Corp., Marriott International, Fannie Mae and Citicorp/Citibank.

He's chairman of the financial advisory committee of TransResources International, the parent company of Haifa Chemical, an Israeli firm.

We ran into Small this week at the Museum of American History. He had turned over the place to Kmart. Kmart and the Smithsonian had become "partners" in bringing to the public a traveling mobile museum featuring a exhibition titled "Wade in the Water: African-American Sacred Music Traditions 1871-2001."

The mobile museum is a 48-foot, double expandable trailer, with giant red Kmart signs emblazoned on each side. The trailer will travel to Kmart stores, schools and elsewhere around the nation.

At the auditorium, Small said that he was "delighted to work with Kmart on this important project" and thanked the retailing giant for its "generous donation."

Brent Willis, Kmart's "chief marketing officer" made some syrupy statement about the benefits of diversity.

We wanted to test Willis' corporate rhetoric against the reality at Kmart.

So we asked Valerie Stokes, Kmart's vice president for human resources, and the company's highest ranking African-American, how many of the company's 300,000 employees were

African American. Stokes said she didn't know. What about a ballpark number? Couldn't tell you. Are any of Kmart's more than 2,100 stores unionized? No. Have there been attempts to unionize? Couldn't tell you.

We asked Small how much money Kmart kicked in to fund the project. "Don't know, you'll have to ask Kmart," Small said. We asked the numerous Kmart spokespeople at the event. Don't know. Can't tell you.

We asked Small why he was turning over the Smithsonian to Kmart, a company with a poor reputation in America, in a corporate public relations effort to burnish its image?

"It's not being used for corporate public relations," Small said.

Then, in the very next breath, he asked, "Why shouldn't they get something out of it? They put up the money for it."

Well, we wanted to know, is it okay for the Smithsonian, which gets two-thirds of its budget from the federal taxpayers, to partner with major American corporations?

At this point, David Umansky, the Smithsonian's director of communications, cuts in.

"I want you to understand something," Umansky says. "The Smithsonian is not a government institution. Write this down. Legislation was passed establishing the Smithsonian Institution as a trust instrumentality of the United States—not the United States government—but the United States. It is not a part of the executive branch, it is not a part of the legislative branch, it is not a part of the judiciary. It is a separate entity."

Got that kids? The Smithsonian gets hundreds of millions of dollars from you and me, and they are before Congress begging for more taxpayer money—and it is not a part of the government.

Umansky wants to know: "Why are you so suspicious?"

Well, there should be a stark dividing line between public and private institutions in America.

You seem to be the only person in America who believes

that, he says.

That would come as a surprise to our readers. We have gotten hundreds of responses from readers who are unhappy with corporate control of public institutions, including when we wrote a couple of years ago about the oil companies taking over a part of the Smithsonian for their exhibit on the Alaska oil pipeline.

You can get hundreds of people upset about the sunrise, Umansky counters.

So, any public institution should be allowed to take private corporate money?

If it's used properly, absolutely, Umansky says. For the Smithsonian, there is no problem.

It's been 20 minutes now, and we still haven't gotten an answer to how much Kmart spent for this little public relations stunt. Umansky doesn't like the persistence. "Why are you being such an asshole?" he asks.

Finally, Umansky gets us an answer on the funding—Kmart put up $2 million in cash and in kind—about $500,000 in cash.

At a press conference at the National Press Club last year, Small was asked about undue corporate influence over the operations of the Smithsonian.

"There is a difference between providing the funding and having an endorsement or having a commercial relationship with the museum," he said. "So, if it's philanthropy, I don't think there's any problem with it."

In this instance, and in many others, the Smithsonian has crossed the line. By allowing the Kmart logo and the Smithsonian logo to be emblazoned all over the press releases, press kits and trailer last week, by giving Kmart's "chief marketing officer" a stage to spout empty corporate platitudes, the Smithsonian Institution was putting its seal of approval on the company.

Every major new exhibit at the Smithsonian over the past

couple of years has been funded by a major American corporation or industry—the Alaska Pipeline exhibit funded by the oil companies, the insect zoo funded by Orkin, and on down the line. The place has become a museum of American corporations.

Earlier this year, an exhibit on the American Presidency, sponsored by Cisco Systems and Chevy Chase Bank, among others, was deemed so important that it had to bump an exhibit on the work of the late folk singer and anti-corporate rabble rouser Woody Guthrie. The Guthrie exhibit was scheduled to run through the spring, but got pulled for the one about the corporate presidency.

Through Small and his predecessors, the corporate state has overtaken the Smithsonian. Congress should take it back for the people.

Congress should demand that as a condition of forking over hundreds of millions of taxpayers' dollars every year, the Smithsonian should kick the corporations out.

It's time to clean house.

Timber Ad Cut

April 3, 2001

We've long accepted as a truism that freedom of the press exists mostly for those who can afford to buy one.

But we assumed that a corollary was that the freedom extended as well to those who could afford to rent one, and buy ads.

That may not be so.

Consider the recent experience of Forest Ethics, a Berkeley, California-based advocacy group that works to protect the ancient rainforests of British Columbia and endangered forests of North America by redirecting U.S. markets toward ecologically sound alternatives.

Campaigns run by coalitions that include Forest Ethics, Rainforest Action Network American Lands Alliance, Forest Action Network, Student Environmental Action Coalition, Earth First!, Greenpeace, Sierra Club, the Natural Resources Defense Council and many others have pressured Home Depot and other major wood sellers to stop selling wood products from old-growth forests. As a result, the timber industry is on the run.

The recalcitrant members of the American Forest & Paper Association have responded to forest activists' successful campaigns and the shifting market for wood by creating their own certification system, the Sustainable Forestry Initiative (SFI). Forest campaigners say SFI is a sham, and are urging wood buyers to give preference to wood certified by the Forest Stewardship Council, an independent organization.

To highlight its concerns with the SFI, Forest Ethics decided to place an advertisement in the Seattle Times during the Green Building Conference, a recent meeting held in Seattle that attracted major U.S. homebuilders.

The group's proposed ad mocked the SFI's claim to represent a "bold approach to sustainable forest management" with a picture of an ancient temperate rainforest clearcut in British

Columbia by the Interfor company, which SFI recently certified as "sustainable." Asking whether SFI was promoting green wood or a greenwash, the Forest Ethics ad also criticized the SFI certification of Boise Cascade. "SFI's endorsement of Boise Cascade, the largest logger of old growth in the U.S., is further evidence of SFI's toothless standards," the ad's text read.

The *Seattle Times* refused to run the ad.

The sticking point, according to Todd Paglia, Forest Ethics campaigns director, was the mention of Interfor and Boise Cascade.

As an aside, we should mention that we are generally not fans of issue advertisements, which we think far too often drain advocacy groups' budgets for little payback, and are a poor substitute for grassroots organizing. But the ads tend to be most effective when used as part of a larger campaign and with the specific purpose of singling out and shaming a particular company or corporate executive.

That is exactly what Forest Ethics intended. Paglia says the Seattle Times offered that the group could run the ad so long as corporations were not mentioned by name. But "at that point, the ad is worthless," Paglia says.

And so the ad didn't run.

The *Seattle Times* disputes Paglia's version of events. Lloyd Stull, national sales manager for the paper, says the Seattle Times only requested documentation to support Forest Ethics' assertions. Paglia insists that the paper was uninterested in either documentation for its claims that the companies' are clearcutting or in suggesting word changes to avert libel concerns.

In any case, we checked on the claims directly. Spokespersons for Interfor and Boise Cascade readily acknowledge the companies are clearcutting. We were not able on short notice to definitively determine whether Boise Cascade is the number one old-growth logger in the United States.

Meanwhile, Forest Ethics directed its attention to the East Coast, and sought to place an ad in the *Boston Globe* targeting

Staples, the office supply company.

"The ugly truth is that thousands of acres of forest are needlessly destroyed every year to supply Staples with cheap, disposable paper products," the proposed ad said.

It urged readers to "call Tom Stemberg [Staples' CEO] at 508-253-7143 and ask him to stop destroying our forests, or send him a fax at www.StopStaples.com. And when Staples tells you they sell hundreds of recycled products, know that in truth 97 percent of their copy paper comes from clearcut forests."

To Paglia's surprise, the *Boston Globe* refused to run the ad. Taking out the phone information was not enough to satisfy the paper—the *Globe* refused to run an ad that mentioned Staples by name. Dennis Lloyd, an advertisement manager at the paper, says only that the paper was not comfortable with the way Forest Ethics "expressed" its views in the ad.

The *New York Times*, by contrast, says that it will run opinion ads so long as they do not constitute libel. A *Times* representative says the paper would have no problem with the substance of the Staples ad and the mention of the company's name.

In recent weeks, right-winger David Horowitz has generated a storm of controversy by seeking to place ads in college newspapers opposing reparations for the descendants of slaves and being refused by some college outlets.

Here's what the *Boston Globe* had to say about the controversy: "The ideas against slavery reparations contained in an advertisement placed in student newspapers around the country may well be insulting to minorities on campus. But they are only ideas. Far more dangerous than offensive ideas is their censorship, because censorship knows no ideology and will Eventually muzzle the views of the minorities as well."

So why the double standard? The *Globe* should be consistent and carry the Forest Ethics ad. The paper's refusal to carry truthful advertisements criticizing corporations mocks the spirit of the First Amendment and the notion that the press will serve as an institutional check on abuses of power.

Every Nook and Cranny

April 24, 2001

We've heard it said that commercialism will keep expanding its frontiers until every boundary has been smashed and non-commercial values are completely extinguished.

Let's now admit that we are rapidly approaching that point.

We are friends with a seven-year-old, who has been sheltered to a large degree from the ravages of commercialism, who likes baseball, and who likes to sing that American classic "Take me out to the Ballgame."

We were driving him to see a major league ballgame the other day, running late, listening to the first inning on the radio, when a jingle for an oil company came on—"Take me Out to Sunoco."

"What's Sunoco?" the seven-year old asked.

"Sun Oil Company," we said in shock.

Slowly, baseball has been giving in to the creep of commercial culture. Of course, for years, ads have played a dominant role at the ballparks. But now things are getting out of control.

Every time the New York Yankees turn a double play, the Yankees play-by-play announcers are required, by contract, to say "There's Another Jiffy Lube Double Play." When Yankee skipper Joe Torre pulls the starting pitcher and calls for a relief pitcher, the Yankees announcers must say there's a "Geico Direct Call to the Bullpen." And so on.

And now, the forces of commercialism have grabbed onto one of baseball's all-time heroes, The Ironman, Lou Gehrig.

Alcatel, the French telecommunications firm that is using Martin Luther King's "I Have a Dream" speech in national television and print ads, has obtained the rights to Gehrig's famous 1939 farewell speech at Yankee Stadium.

In that speech, despite having a fatal disease that bears his name—amyotrophic lateral sclerosis—Gehrig told the Yankee stadium crowd on that day he considered himself "the luckiest man on the face of the Earth."

We called up Brian Murphy, the U.S. spokesperson for Alcatel and asked him about the Gehrig ad. He said that decision on whether to run the ad would be made within a few weeks.

We made the point that Dr. King was not about commercialism and would never have allowed his name to be used for commercial purposes.

We reminded Murphy that there has been strong criticism from the civil rights community over the use of Dr. King to sell the French company's telephone equipment.

On the Today Show last month, Julian Bond, chairman of the NAACP and a colleague of Dr. King's, ripped into Alcatel.

"It just seems to me that some things ought to be sacrosanct," Bond said. "Some things ought not be commercialized. Martin Luther King is one of those icons of the movement. This just strikes me as leading us further and further down a dangerous path. I can imagine some day seeing Franklin Roosevelt saying, 'We have nothing to fear but headache pain,' or John F. Kennedy saying, 'Ask not what you can do for your country, but what you could do for Country Ham.' It just strikes me as a further intrusion of commercialism into some of the—one of the most important icons of the 20th century."

Murphy admitted that the company has received "mixed reactions" to the King, but defended the company's course, reminding us that the King estate was paid for the rights to the "I Have a Dream" speech.

How much? We asked.

"That's proprietary information," he said.

"We worked with the King Foundation, the King estate throughout the process, they approved the King ad—all along we wanted to make sure we were honoring Dr. King and we feel we did," Murphy said. "We believe we did the right thing."

But what about the fact that Dr. King would never have allowed such a thing, that he was disappointed that our country had failed "to deal positively and forthrightly with the triple evils of racism, extreme materialism and militarism."

"I don't know the man," Murphy blurted out.

Clearly you don't.

Censorship at the
National Press Club

June 22, 2001

Henry Kissinger came to the National Press Club here in Washington, D.C. last night to give a talk, sell his latest book, Does America Need a Foreign Policy? and take questions from an audience of about 300 people.

We weren't as interested in the talk or the book as much as the question period. We figured, correctly as it turned out, that Henry hadn't change over the years—his unspoken theory of foreign policy was still the same: the corporate state—including his client corporations—should dictate the country's foreign policy. As usual, his words barely masked that reality.

But scattered throughout the ballroom at the Press Club were little white note cards for questions, and it appeared that perhaps 100 questions were scribbled and sent up to the moderator, Richard Koonce, a member of the Press Club's book and author committee.

It was Koonce's job to sift through the questions, pick out some interesting ones, and ask Henry some probing questions. This system seemed to work well at luncheon talks, where the past three presidents of the Press Club—Doug Harbrecht of *Business Week*, John Cushman of the *New York Times* and Dick Ryan of the *Detroit News*—would ask speakers some pretty tough and newsworthy questions. We never got the sense that Press Club moderators were pulling punches.

Last night, things changed.

Earlier this year, *Harper's* magazine published a two-part series of articles by British journalist Christopher Hitchens, "The Case Against Henry Kissinger that has since been published as a book, *The Trial of Henry Kissinger* (Verso).

Hitchens has drawn up an indictment, charged Kissinger with war crimes, and is begging some government to go after the former Secretary of State under Richard Nixon for the killings of innocents in Laos, Cambodia, South America, East Timor and elsewhere.

Magistrates in three countries—Chile, Argentina, and France—have responded and summoned Kissinger to answer questions.

Le Monde reported earlier this month that when French Judge Roger Le Loire had a summons served on Kissinger on May 31 at the Ritz Hotel in Paris, Kissinger promptly left the hotel, and then left town. The judge wanted to ask Kissinger about his knowledge of Operation Condor, an effort by the dictators of South America to kill or "disappear" dissidents.

The fact that Kissinger was being sought for questioning didn't make the mainstream media here in the United States, until yesterday's *New York Times* reported that the Chilean judge wanted Kissinger to "testify about the disappearance of an American in Chile when the dictator Augusto Pinochet seized power in the 1970s."

Kissinger began lashing back at Hitchens last week, not by answering the substance of Hitchen's argument, but by smearing the journalist.

Kissinger told Detroit radio talk show host Mitch Albom that Hitchens had "denied the Holocaust ever took place."

In response, Hitchens, who says both and he his wife are Jewish, told the *New York Post*: "Mr. Kissinger will be hearing from my attorney, who will tell him two things he already knows—what he said is false, malicious and defamatory, and if he says it again, we will proceed against him in court."

So, you can imagine that the Press Club audience had questions. And so did we.

We wrote down six questions—about the report in the *Times*, Kissinger's interview with Albom, the incident at the Ritz Hotel in Paris, Hitchen's articles in Harper's, about the three magistrates and simply this one: "If you are indicted for war crimes, will you defend yourself in court?"

We met a friend there who told us that in the 1970s, when

Kissinger was asked about the bombing of Laos and Cambodia, he responded this way: "sometimes we have to operate outside the law."

Her question to Kissinger: "How do you square that with our Constitutional values?"

Koonce had other ideas. He lofted six or seven puffballs about Kissinger in China, about Kissinger on Nixon, about his generic views of foreign policy. Nothing about war crimes, nothing about operating outside the law, nothing about Hitchens.

After the event, we sought out Koonce.

"Was there an agreement with Dr. Kissinger not to ask questions related to Christopher Hitchens and allegations of war crimes?"

To our surprise, Koonce did not deny it.

"There was a definite sensitivity to that," Koonce said. "He [Kissinger] was afraid that if we got into a discussion of that, for the vast majority of people that, it would take so much time to explain all of the context, that you know, he preferred to avoid that, and so . . ."

And so Kissinger's wishes were accommodated and the questions were avoided.

We asked Koonce how many written questions dealt with Hitchens or war crimes? Two or three, Koonce said.

We knew this not to be true. We handed up six ourselves. And we suspect that there were many more. (Only Kissinger knows for sure, since it's Press Club policy to deliver the written questions to the guest after the event.)

According to Press Club standards, these book events must be held in accordance with the Club's "Code of Ethics."

So, we want to know—how can it be ethical to agree secretly with an author before hand not to ask a certain set of questions?

We're tracking down the Code of Ethics. Stay tuned.

Slam the Doctor's Door on the Pharmaceutical Companies

July 6, 2001

We walked out of our office the other day and almost tripped over a little white shopping bag. We looked up and down the corridor, and there were little white shopping bags in front of every door. Somebody wanted to send a message to the reporters in the National Press Building.

That somebody was a joint venture between Johnson & Johnson and Merck. The message: use our new Pepcid antacid to fight heartburn.

In the little white shopping bag was a 100 percent cotton blue t-shirt with the message "Make the Pepcid Complete Switch" on the front and "Pepcid Complete—We've got heartburn surrounded" on the back.

Also in the bag was a sample of Pepcid Complete and a hand sized plastic chile pepper that informs us that Pepcid complete "starts to neutralize acid in seconds and last seven times longer than Tums." (Glaxosmithkline, the maker of Tums, is suing Johnson & Johnson Merck Consumer Pharmaceutical Co. the maker of Pepcid Complete, for disparaging Tums in a television commercial.)

And then there was a press release, inviting all reporters to the Ninth Annual National Capital Barbecue Battle.

The idea was this: get reporters to come and eat the BBQ, and blazing hot peppers, give them all heartburn, and then force feed them Pepcid "so revelers can experience fast and long-lasting heartburn relief."

That's the M.O. of the drug companies these days—get people sick so that they can make money treating them.

The drug companies have flipped out in their drive for greater profit margins. They are pushing their drugs into every nook and cranny of society.

This despite compelling evidence that many of the new

drugs being developed are unnecessary, dangerous, or both.

Our doctor friend, Matt Hahn, who practices in rural West Virginia, gets 10 to 20 drug reps a day visiting him in an effort to try and persuade him and his staff to buy new drugs and take samples. (Imagine the traffic jam faced in the offices of big city doctors.)

These drug reps offend Dr. Hahn and hundreds of other doctors who believe that much of our suffering—from high blood pressure, diabetes, emphysema and lung cancer—is preventable if we exercise, eat the right foods, and stop smoking.

We could cut out a big chunk of drug expenditures if we practiced prevention. This still empty threat of a national prevention program keeps the drug reps on their toes. Imagine what such a program would do the GNPP (gross national pharmaceutical product)?

Dr. Hahn would ban these drug reps from his clinic, but he actually can use some of the more useful samples—especially the antibiotics—for his patients who can't afford the drug companies exorbitant prices.

He has tried to put the kibosh on the most obnoxious drug reps. These include the diabetes drug reps, who come bearing fat-laden pizzas for Dr. Hahn's staff—exactly the kind of food that if eaten regularly triggers weight gain and diabetes.

Dr. Hahn says that out of the hundreds of diabetes patients he has treated, he has never met one who eats well and exercises regularly. And, he says, the drug reps carrying diabetes samples just don't get the irony of their bringing the junk food into the office.

Dr. Hahn understands that these drug reps leave the free food, drink and drug samples, not out of the generosity of the drug companies, but to influence the doctor's future behavior. And he knows about the studies that prove how these gifts, free dinners, and vacation junkets the drug reps throw at doctors and their families influence doctor behavior.

A January 2001 article in the *Journal of the American*

Medical Association, for example, reported that researchers reviewed 538 studies on the topic and concluded that marketing does influence which drugs doctors prescribe and which they ask to be included on hospitals' list of preferred drugs.

"These kinds of inducements are fundamentally problematic," says Dr. Paul Wolpe, a fellow at the University of Pennsylvania's Center for Bioethics. "They are ill-conceived bribes to get more attention of physicians than their rivals."

We like Dr. Hahn's prevention program, which must play a central role in addressing our current health care disaster. But it's a long term program that must start with young people.

In the short term, so that doctors can practice in peace and in a fat free environment, let's slam the doctor's door on the pharmaceutical companies.

The Age of Inequality

May 28, 2002

Here's the latest evidence of the startling growth of income and wealth inequality, in the United States and around the world:

The *Washington Post's* Ceci Connolly reports this week on the development of a new innovation in healthcare delivery: "boutique" or "concierge" coverage for the world's super-elite.

Leading medical providers like the Cleveland Clinic and Johns Hopkins in Baltimore are establishing special programs to give platinum service to the well-heeled. Depending on the program, the super-rich customers may receive massages and sauna time along with their physical, housecalls, and step-to-the-front-of-the-line service in testing facilities.

Using these services are a worldwide elite class of business executives and royalty—the "winners" in a system of corporate globalization that is generating morally repugnant economic disparities.

Here are some other measures of the gains of the wealthy:

- Executive pay at top U.S. corporations climbed 571 percent from 1990 to 2000.
- There are presently nearly 500 billionaires worldwide.
- U.S. corporate tax payments are slated to drop to historic lows as a result of the tax bill enacted into law earlier this year. According to Citizens for Tax Justice, corporate taxes will plummet to only 1.3 percent of U.S. gross domestic product this year, the lowest since fiscal 1983, and the second lowest level in the last 60 years.
- More than half of the tax cuts enacted last year that are scheduled to take effect after 2002 will go to the best-off 1 percent of all U.S. taxpayers.

Even in the United States—the nation that is supposed to be the biggest winner from globalization—the average person has watched skyrocketing executive compensation and wealth accumulation, but has not been able to climb even a few steps up the economic ladder. Average real wages in the United States are at or below the wage rate of 1973.

Meanwhile, poverty remains pervasive in both the United States and around the world.

- One in six children in the United States live in poverty.
- In 2000, a full quarter of the U.S. population was earning poverty-level wages, according to the Economics Policy Institute.
- Around the world, 1.2 billion persons live on a dollar a day, or less.
- Tens of millions of children worldwide are locked out of school because their parents are unable to afford school fees.
- More than a million children die a year form diarrhea, because their families lack access to clean drinking water.

The Institute for Policy Studies has sought to put these disparities into perspective. The 497 billionaires in 2001 registered a combined wealth of $1.54 trillion, according to IPS, well over the combined gross national products of all the nations of sub-Saharan Africa ($929.3 billion) or those of the oil-rich regions of the Middle East and North Africa ($1.34 trillion). "This collective wealth of the 497 is also greater than the combined incomes of the poorest half of humanity," IPS concludes.

It's not very easy to wrap one's mind around the inhumanity of these numbers.

That is why it is so important to highlight anecdotes that put the problem in focus: the juxtaposition of concierge health-care with the more than 40 million people in the United States who have no health insurance coverage at all, the contrast between the boutique care and the more than a million children dying each year because they don't have clean water to drink.

Sometimes, we need to recognize obscene social arrangements for what they are, and demand something different.

Why *Newsweek* is Bad for Kids

Did you see the cover story of *Newsweek* magazine last week?

The cover story is titled, "Why TV is Good for Kids."

What are we to expect from *Newsweek* next week?

Why Soda Pop is Good for Kids.

Why Sedentary Living is Good for Kids.

Why Obesity is Good for Kids.

Some things are good for kids.

Reading is good for kids.

Love and caring is good for kids.

Teaching is good for kids.

Running, playing basketball and baseball and tennis and swimming are good for kids.

But don't try and insult us by telling us that sitting in front of a TV is good for kids.

Why, against all common sense, is Newsweek going to try and convince us that television is good for kids?

Well, one reason might be: *Newsweek* is owned by the *Washington Post* Company, which owns a sprawling cable company and six broadcast stations around the country.

Of course, nowhere in the article does Newsweek tell us this.

And how does *Newsweek* try and convince us that TV is good for kids?

They trot out an expert, Daniel Anderson, a professor of psychology at the University of Massachusetts, who claims that TV is good for kids.

But what *Newsweek* doesn't tell us is Anderson is a paid consultant to a variety of television networks and advertising interests.

His clients include: NBC, CBS, Universal Pictures, Sony, General Mills, the Leo Burnett ad agency, Nickelodeon and the

National Association of Broadcasters.

The article says that TV is a good thing because kids learn from television and parents are "looking for TV to help them do a better job of raising kids."

But Frank Vespe, executive director of the TV TurnOff Network (www.tvturnoff.org), points out that the article misses a crucial issue: the average American school child spends more time in front of the television each year—about 1,023 hours—than in the classroom—about 900 hours.

"This amount of television—more than twice what anyone thinks is a healthy amount—has negative consequences for health, education, and family time," Vespe said.

This amount of television watching actually hurts children.

Vespe points to studies documenting how kids gain weight from watching TV, and that TV reinforces sex roles and stereotyping.

Voracious TV-watching kids turn into voracious TV-watching adults. The average American watches four hours a day, 1460 hours a year, about two full months, 24 hours a day, every year.

Newsweek did run a one-page counterpoint ("No It's Not") to its "TV Is Good for Kids" eight pager.

The "No It's Not" counterarticle is written by a mom who points out that the American Academy of Pediatrics recommends no television for children younger than two and a maximum of two hours a day of "screen time"—TV, computers or videogames—for older kids.

We rang up the author of the "Why TV Is Good for Kids" article, Daniel McGinn.

McGinn immediately points out that at the end of his article, he did write that the expert, Anderson, advised on a handful of television shows during their conception.

"People who help create television shows get paid to do so," McGinn tells us.

Well, yes, but Anderson gets paid to do much more.

According to his own bio, Anderson has been paid by NBC and by General Mills to consult "on television viewing behavior."

And he's been paid by the Leo Burnett ad agency to consult on "children's cognitive processing of television."

That's a touch more than helping to "create television shows."

We asked *Newsweek*'s McGinn why he didn't inform his readers that Newsweek is owned by the Washington Post which owns a cable company and six broadcast news outlets.

"*Newsweek* is owned by the *Washington Post*," he says. "I'm not sure what the *Washington Post* owns today."

You mean you don't know that the *Washington Post* Company owns television outlets?

It's right on the company's web site: WDIV in Detroit, KPRC in Houston, WPLG in Miami, WKMP in Orlando, KSAT in San Antonio and WJXT in Jacksonville.

The Post also owns Cable ONE, the owner and operator of cable television systems serving subscribers across the country.

Earlier, McGinn left a message on our machine saying he was willing to talk with us "at whatever length."

At this point, though, McGinn decides the conversation has gone on long enough.

"Who do you write for?" he asks. We tell him.

"Have a great day, bud." And he hangs up.

Corporations:
Different Than You and Me

January 24, 2001

Corporations are fundamentally different than you and me.

That's a simple truth that Big Business leaders desperately hope the public will not perceive.

It helps companies immeasurably that the law in the United States and in many other countries confers upon them the same rights as human beings.

In the United States, this personhood treatment, established most importantly in a throwaway line in an 1886 Supreme Court decision, protects the corporate right to advertise (including the tobacco companies' right to market their deadly wares), corporations' ability to contribute monetarily to political campaigns, and interferes with regulators' facility inspection rights (via corporate rights against unreasonable search and seizure).

But even more important than the legal protections gained by faux personhood status are the political, social and cultural benefits.

Companies aggressively portray themselves as part of the community (every community), a friendly neighbor. If they succeed in that effort at self-characterization, they know what follows: a dramatically diminished likelihood of external constraints on their operations. If a corporation is part of the community, then it is entitled to the same freedoms available to others, and the same presumption of non-interference that society appropriately affords real people.

Especially because corporations work so aggressively and intentionally to obscure the point, it is crucial to draw attention to the corporation as an institution with unique powers, motivations and attributes, and to point to the basic differences between human beings and the socially constituted and authorized institutions called corporations.

Here are 10 differences between corporations and real people:

1. Corporations have perpetual life.

2. Corporations can be in two or more places at the same time.

3. Corporations cannot be jailed.

4. Corporations have no conscience or sense of shame.

5. Corporations have no sense of altruism, nor willingness to adjust their behavior to protect future generations.

6. Corporations pursue a single-minded goal, profit, and are typically legally prohibited from seeking other ends.

7. There are no limits, natural or otherwise, to corporations' potential size.

8. Because of their political power, they are able to define or at very least substantially affect, the civil and criminal regulations that define the boundaries of permissible behavior. Virtually no individual criminal has such abilities.

9. Corporations can combine with each other, into bigger and more powerful entities.

10. Corporations can divide themselves, shedding subsidiaries or affiliates that are controversial, have brought them negative publicity or pose liability threats.

These unique attributes give corporations extraordinary power, and makes the challenge of checking their power all the more difficult. The institutions are much more powerful than individuals, which makes all the more frightening their single-minded profit maximizing efforts.

Corporations have no conscience, or has been famously said, no soul. As a result, they exercise little self-restraint. Exacerbating the problem, because they have no conscience, many of the sanctions we impose on individuals-not just imprisonment, but the more important social norms of shame and community disapproval-have limited relevance to or impact on corporations.

The fact that corporations are not like us, their very unique characteristics, makes crucially important the development of an array of controls on corporations. These include: precise limits on corporate behaviors (such as actively enforced environmental, consumer, worker safety regulations); limits on corporate size and power (through vigorous antitrust and pro-competition policy, including limits on the scope of intellectual property protections); restrictions and prohibitions on corporate political activity (including through comprehensive campaign finance reform); carefully tailored civil and criminal sanctions responsive to the particular traits of corporations including denying wrongdoing companies the ability to bid for government contracts; equity fines-fines paid in stock, not dollars; creative probation, with a court-appointed ombudsman given authority to order specific changes in corporate activities; and restrictions on corporations' ability to close or move facilities.

There is also the permanent challenge of building countervailing centers of people power to balance concentrated corporate power: unions above all, plus consumer, environmental, indigenous rights and other civic groups, organized in conventional and novel formations.

And there is the imperative of directly confronting the corporate claim to personhood and community neighbor status-both in the law and in the broader culture.

This is the beginning of a sketch of an ambitious agenda, but there is no alternative, if democracy is to be rescued from the corporate hijackers who masquerade as everyday citizens.

The Moral of the Story: Care

December 19, 2001

The Supreme Court says a corporation is a person, or at least must be treated like one when it comes to most constitutional protections.

These protections include the right to speak and the right to act in the political arena—giving campaign contributions, lobbying, and advocating its agenda.

Now, if a corporation is in fact a person, with full constitutional rights, then it should act like a moral human person.

And what is the fundamental basis of morality? Caring about others.

So, a corporation, to act like a moral human person, is going to have to care about others, not just about its own bottom line.

It is going to have to care about its human compatriots.

But the vast majority of major corporations don't give a damn about their fellow persons. As such, they are immoral—or amoral—to the core.

We say, if you are not a human person, and you can't act like a moral human person, then you should be stripped of your constitutional protections.

No right to speak, no Fifth Amendment rights, no right to participate in the political arena. You just produce your products and go home.

It also makes sense to revisit the legal protections that facilitate corporate im- or a-morality, particularly the corporation's defining characteristic—limited liability for shareholders.

Shareholders, the owners of a corporation, invest a certain amount of money in a company. Under the rules of limited liability, no matter how much harm the company does, or how much it owes creditors, shareholders cannot be required to pay more than the amount they already put in.

Lawrence Mitchell, a professor of law at George

Washington University, believes that limited liability for share-holders leads shareholders—and therefore corporations—not to care. If your liability is limited, you won't care as much as if your liability is full.

"We call stockholders owners," Mitchell said recently. "You can hardly be considered an owner if you don't care, if you don't act like it's your property. Limited liability encourages stockholders not to care."

Mitchell, who has written a book, *Corporate Irresponsibility: America's Newest Export* (Yale University Press, 2001), says that in the absence of limited liability, the corporation can always buy insurance.

"Insurance internalizes the cost of the risk," Mitchell said. "The corporation has to pay based on the insurance company's assessment of the risk, rather than some creditor getting stuck holding the bag if the corporation fails."

So, yes, Mitchell would strip corporations of their limited liability protection. Let the chips fall where they may.

Admittedly, these ideas don't appear likely to be implemented soon. But there may be interim concepts to get us closer.

A first step would be to take away constitutional protections and limited liability from the worst-acting corporations.

To determine whether a corporation is acting morally, we propose that Congress legislate a Corporate Character Commission (CCC). This would be a 10-person panel, with members chosen from the human person community. Ideal candidates would be ethicists, philosophers, corporate criminologists and the like. The CCC would check on the criminal records, recidivism rates, acts of immorality and other wrongdoing of the largest corporations.

There is a precedent for this kind of review at the federal level. The Federal Communications Commission reviews the character of applicants for federal broadcast licenses. The FCC does not do a very good job of it, obviously. General Electric, for example, routinely gets renewed despite its recidivist record.

But just because the FCC can't do it right, doesn't mean the CCC couldn't do it right.

Now, you are probably saying to yourself? Yeah, right? Hell will freeze over first before Congress creates such a Commission.

The CCC would be a modest step to a future where the corporations are subservient to moral human beings, where caring for others takes precedence over the bottom line, where you and I matter than Enron and Boeing.

Advertise This!

September 6, 2002

Corporations are gaining ground fast in their effort to assume all of the U.S. constitutional protections afforded human beings.

Some of the last limitations on corporate free speech rights may be about to fall, thanks to Supreme Court decisions that increasingly equate commercial advertising with political speech, and a Food and Drug Administration (FDA) that appears eager to accept Court-imposed restrictions on its authority.

To see what you can do to help block this corporate empowerment, see: http://www.essentialaction.org/commercial-speech.

An 1886 Supreme Court decision established that corporations in the United States are entitled to constitutional protections. Since then, the Court has progressively extended Bill of Rights protections, including First Amendment speech rights, and other constitutional guarantees to corporations. In 1978, the Court established a constitutional right to "commercial speech"—speech intended to promote and advertise products for sale, as opposed to political or expressive speech.

Since 1978, the courts have steadily expanded commercial speech rights, taking a potentially dramatic step in a decision issued earlier this year.

In that decision, Thompson v. Western States Medical Center, the Supreme Court interpreted its commercial speech test, developed in a case called Central Hudson, to make it very difficult for the government to restrict commercial speech.

Western States Medical Center involved a provision of a 1997 law that permits pharmacies to make compounded pharmaceuticals—drugs manufactured on the premises, to serve the specific needs of particular patients. The 1997 law permits compounded drugs to be sold—even though they have not passed

FDA safety and efficacy tests—but on condition that they not be advertised. The basic idea is to seek a balance: to permit manufacture for specifically prescribed needs, but to prevent pharmacies from circumventing the FDA's safety rules by advertising untested compounded drugs to the broad public.

The Supreme Court struck down this provision, holding that it violated the commercial speech rights of the pharmacies. In conducting the Central Hudson test, the Court agreed that there is a substantial governmental interest in protecting public health and preserving the integrity of the FDA drug approval process, and conceded the advertising restrictions might directly advance these ends. But it held that the law failed to satisfy the final prong of the Central Hudson test, "whether it is not more extensive than necessary to serve that interest."

Justice O'Connor, writing for the majority, posited a series of alternatives to an ad ban, without citing any evidence, or even providing compelling arguments, that these alternatives would work as effectively as an ad ban. But they were enough for the majority to conclude that the advertising restrictions were more extensive than necessary.

This holding seems to move the Central Hudson test away from ascertaining whether there is a reasonable fit between the government's commercial speech regulations and its legitimate goals, and towards a much higher level of scrutiny. The Court is beginning to break down the constitutional distinction between political and (nonmisleading) commercial speech—even though commercial speech protections essentially apply uniquely to corporations, which do most commercial advertising.

The Supreme Court justifies this rising level of protection for commercial speech on the grounds that the government cannot legitimately deny the public truthful commercial information to prevent the public from making bad decisions with the information.

But why not?

If the Court is going to justify commercial speech protections based on the public's right to know, as opposed to the speaker's right to speak, it makes sense for the government to make determinations about whether the commercial information actually will educate the public to advance public policy goals. It is hardly a revelation that advertising contains promotional elements that may drown out its educational benefits.

The high level of protection afforded to commercial speech by the courts poses a difficult challenge for regulatory agencies that reasonably seek to restrict advertising, including and especially the FDA, which has good public health reasons to restrict advertising and promotional claims.

For example, drug companies now spend billions of dollars a year on Direct-to-Consumer (DTC) prescription drug advertising, with more spent to advertise leading drug brands than Pepsi or Budweiser. These ads encourage consumers to demand, and doctors to prescribe, pharmaceuticals that people don't need. The ads fail to convey the comparative benefits of the marketed drugs to alternatives. They don't reveal price information.

DTC ads should be prohibited. But as long as the Supreme Court holds that there are constitutional speech protections, they must be highly regulated. Now, the extent of FDA's authority to regulate DTC ads is somewhat uncertain.

Or consider tobacco (not currently under the jurisdiction of the FDA, or any federal health agency). There is an abundance of studies conclusively showing that advertising increases smoking rates, especially among youth. Tobacco ads and promotions should be banned. Commercial speech protections make this impossible. The Court's new formulation may also make even more modest restrictions on tobacco promotion very difficult.

There is no question that the Court has made things hard for the FDA, which must maneuver to give itself the greatest possible latitude to restrict advertising to protect public health.

Unfortunately, the FDA seems quite happy to forfeit the

powers it needs to do its job. In May, the agency put out a request for comments (with a comment period open until mid-September) on issues involving First Amendment protections for commercial speech and the scope of the agency's authority. It appears the agency is looking for excuses to throw up its hands—"Sure, we'd like to do our job, but there's not much we can do. The Supreme Court says corporations have a constitutional right to advertise, even if that will harm public health."

The outcome, however, is not a foregone conclusion. Twenty-five years ago, there were no constitutional protections for commercial speech. The tide can be turned back, beginning with a public demand that the Food and Drug Administration—the leading U.S. public health regulatory agency—assert the supremacy of protecting the public health over a purported constitutional right for corporations to hawk their wares.

Licensed to Kill, Inc.

April 21, 2003

There is a new tobacco company in town, and it aims to teach a lesson or two.

The company: Licensed to Kill, Inc.

Licensed to Kill, Inc. is incorporated in the state of Virginia, for the explicit purpose of engaging "in any business permitted by the Commonwealth of Virginia and not required to be stated herein including, but not limited to, the manufacture and marketing of tobacco products in a way that each year kills over 400,000 Americans and 4.5 million other persons worldwide." (You can view the articles of incorporation at: <http://www.licensedtokill.biz/articles.html>.)

"We're not like other tobacco companies that try to obscure what their business is about," says the company's short introduction, published on its website <www.licensedtokill.biz>. "If you market cigarettes, you market death. It's that simple. In a country which effectively allows corporations to be formed without regard to their purpose, corporations are allowed to kill people to make money. Addiction to cigarettes may be lethal, but profiting from spreading death is perfectly legal."

Describing its unique identity, the company states, 'The name 'Licensed to Kill' is truly a tobacco name—a name associated with leadership in corporate killing in that industry in the United States and around the world. We do not own any companies that are not tobacco-based, and we do not feel a need to purchase any food subsidiaries to obscure the fact that our prime source of profit is indeed cigarettes. By taking such a name, Licensed to Kill, Inc clearly identifies what it is: a company that has been given the explicit permission by the state to manufacture and market tobacco products in a way that each year kills over 400,000 Americans and 4.5 million other persons worldwide. In short, a company that profits off of some of the world's most deadly brands."

"Some have speculated that the choice of the name 'Licensed to Kill' is perhaps a tad bit too truthful. It isn't. Licensed to Kill, Inc. takes pride in owning what we believe to be the premier tobacco company in the world. Going forward, our identity will give stakeholders clarity about the purpose of our company."

Taking a jab at Philip Morris, which has renamed its holding company Altria, Licensed to Kill, Inc. says, "We don't hide what our business is really about behind an altruistic-sounding name."

Why was such a company created?

Licensed to Kill, Inc. is the inspiration of Robert Hinkley, a former corporate lawyer now turned activist, and is a project of Essential Action.

It was formed to make a point both about corporations generally, and the tobacco industry in particular.

States once exercised a modicum of control—and retain the power to exercise real control—over the incorporation, or corporate chartering process. Corporations are creatures of the state. States have the authority, through their chartering process and through corporations law, to establish rules setting boundaries on corporate conduct and requiring certain kinds of corporate activity.

Over the years, however, states have effectively forfeited these powers, though they remain dormant and could be reasserted.

Underlying the creation of Licensed to Kill, Inc. was this question: Have states made the incorporation process so pro forma that they would grant a charter to a company that set out as its purpose the killing of millions of people a year?

Now we know the answer: Yes.

The idea of highlighting such an extreme example—that a literal parody could gain a charter—is to suggest how out of control the chartering process has become, and to suggest that it is time to reimpose controls.

Of course, although it is a parody, Licensed to Kill, Inc.'s business plan differs from the actual business plans of existing tobacco companies in only one notable respect: Its willingness to acknowledge the deadly, devastating impacts of the industry's marketing practices, product manipulation, manipulation and misrepresentation of science, political influence buying, and fundamental way of doing business.

Nearly 5 million people a year worldwide are now dying from tobacco-related disease, thanks in considerable part to the way the industry chooses to do business.

A choice the companies have, because the states fail to impose basic controls on the companies they authorize to do business.

The bottom line message conveyed by License to Kill, Inc.: No one—and certainly no corporation—should have a license to kill. And any system that is willing to grant one is fundamentally flawed, and should be scrapped.

'CHRISTINE TODD WHITMAN, PLEASE... SAY, CHRISTINE, I'VE BEEN HEARING SOME VERY CONVINCING ARGUMENTS ABOUT THE POSITIVE ASPECTS OF CARBON DIOXIDE...'

3/15

PART FIVE

FRONTING FOR BIG BUSINESS

By the mid-1970s, Big Business realized it had a serious problem in the United States: popular movements in the streets, combined with a growing legion of public interest organizations, mostly based in Washington, D.C., were forcing through legislation and major policy changes that were driving up costs and infringing on their ability to act as they pleased.

A 1973 memo from Lewis Powell, a corporate lawyer who would go on to serve on the Supreme Court, issued a call to action. The citizens were growing increasingly organized and boisterous, Powell said. It was time for corporations to organize themselves, too.

Soon, Big Business was revitalizing the staid trade associations in Washington. Corporations began throwing money at right-wing thinktanks such as the Heritage Foundation to issue an endless stream of studies, statements and news releases supporting the corporate line. Corporations and industries began relying on public relations firms. And the business class began investing ever-increasing amounts in lobbyists and political campaigns.

For almost any contested legislative or regulatory issue concerning business practices, business interests now run a full-fledged advocacy campaign. By the 1990s, these campaigns routinely featured the use of front groups—corporate lobbies disguised to look like citizen groups—which work effectively to confuse politicians and the media as to how citizen groups view an issue.

But one thing is even better than relying on artificial creations to serve as fronts: coopting what were once genuine public interest groups to advance the corporate line. There's no complicated explanation of how this happens: public interest groups are generally poor, and corporations have lots of cash.

There are degrees, of course. Some groups sell their soul, and their good name, to an array of corporations. Others restrict the kinds of corporate funding they take and under what conditions. But corporations are not charitable entities: when they make a donation, they generally expect to get something back.

Keep the "Public" in Public Health

August 6, 1999

The great thing about the American Public Health Association (APHA) is in its name—it's about public health—what we as a society do to assure the conditions in which people can be healthy.

If we were to choose a steward for the public health, we would, without hesitation, choose the APHA over, say, the American Medical Association (AMA).

In one sad example in 1997, the AMA cut a deal to endorse Sunbeam medical products in return for royalty payments in the millions. This policy seemed to say, "Not only are we in favor of turning health care over to for-profit corporations, we are in favor of turning our organization over to for-profit corporations." (Following a huge public outcry, that deal was eventually rescinded and the AMA vice president who cut the deal resigned in disgrace.)

But it is the APHA which stands for public health.

We were thinking about this the other day, walking past APHA's gorgeous new $13 million headquarters building in the Chinatown section of Washington, D.C. We went into the lobby, said hello to the staff, and picked up the annual report.

Wherein, we learned that earlier this year, the APHA accepted a $1 million grant from Colgate Palmolive, that consumer giant that brings you Colgate toothpaste, Irish Spring soap, Palmolive dishwashing soap, Speed Stick deodorant.

According to the annual report, the money was used, in part, to launch a national public health education campaign, "Lather Up for Good Health." Under the campaign, APHA and Colgate Palmolive distributed 100,000 "handwashing posters."

At a press conference in Washington, D.C. last week, we ran into Mohammed Akhter, APHA's executive director.

We wanted to know what he thought Colgate Palmolive's interest was in donating $200,000 a year over five years.

"We do not accept money with any strings attached," Akhter said. "They gave us the money to do education about maternal-child health."

"So they get nothing directly," Akhter said. "They gave us the money to do education about maternal-child health. So, one interest is goodwill—the company gets on the good side of mothers and children. And through this they sell more of their products—toothpaste, soaps and such."

Isn't he concerned about undue influence of a giant private corporation over an organization designed to promote "public" health?

"Business is America," Akhter said. "America's whole structure is built on business. But we say that if there are funds that come to us from a corporation that has a bad environmental record, has poor public health practices, poor occupational practices, poor labor practices, we will not accept the money. Or if there is a string attached, we will not accept the money. If someone tells me, 'Sell my sugar and I will give you a million dollars,' I will say no."

Akhter said that he was approached recently by GlaxoWellcome. The multinational pharmaceutical giant wanted to donate $100,000 a year for two or three years.

Akhter said that Glaxo's involvement with the drug industry's efforts to block widespread use of HIV/AIDS drugs in the Third World eliminated the company from consideration. "We said we will not do this," Akhter said. "Don't come to us looking for support for this drug issue."

Akhter said that Eli Lilly has given $30,000 or so a year for a number of years. And Merck donates the bags to carry the programs and other materials for APHA's 30,000 members at its annual convention.

Many members of APHA are concerned about the organization's upcoming first ever fund raising campaign to help pay for the building and APHA's $12 million a year budget.

Frank Goldsmith, professor of health policy at SUNY

Stony Brook, is a former APHA executive board member. Goldsmith believes that APHA should build the organization, not by raking in corporate dollars, but by aggressively pushing a public health agenda and bringing in new members.

"I'm not opposed to getting five or ten thousand from companies who are involved in health care as nutritional organizations, or as food organizations, or insurance companies," he told us. "But when you start talking about hundreds of thousands of dollars or millions, then that becomes a big chunk of the budget and that becomes a problem. You start relying on that money. And APHA executive board members, well-meaning public health people who are worried about the survival of their organization, will be swayed to take the money and take the organization in a direction away from public health."

Akhter said that he heard from "less than 2 percent of the membership" after news of the Colgate Palmolive $1 million grant broke telling him, "be careful."

"Nobody said, 'We don't want the money.' They said, 'Be careful. APHA is not for sale.'"

But we are concerned that by accepting the $1 million from Colgate Palmolive, the message has been sent: if not for sale, then for rent.

Fronting for Big Coal

July 11, 2000

So, we're sitting in our office, and under the door comes a note advising us that there will be a press conference the next day where African-American and Hispanic groups will release a report showing how minority populations will suffer most if the United Nations Global Warming Treaty (Kyoto agreement) passes the U.S. Senate.

The press conference was being pulled together by Advantage Communications Consultants, a public relations firm in Houston, and coordinated by a group called the Center for Energy and Economic Development (CEED).

A simple check tells us that CEED is a coal industry front group. Of course, the coal industry has a lot to lose if the United States moves away from fossil fuels and toward renewable energy sources, like solar.

But nothing in the press materials tells us that this is a coal industry event. So we decide to go to the press conference and play along.

And it's a slow news day, so when we arrive, there are many reporters attending the press briefing, including reporters from the Associated Press and *Los Angeles Times*. C-SPAN's camera is there to beam the press conference out live.

And the moderator, Linda Brown, from the Houston public relations firm, makes her opening statement, saying Blacks and Hispanics are left out of the national policy debate on global warming.

We are told that six Black and Hispanic groups, including the AFL-CIO's A. Phillip Randolph Institute, the National Black Chamber of Commerce, and the United States Hispanic Chamber of Commerce, are releasing a report.

The report finds that "millions of blacks, Hispanics and other minorities could be pushed into poverty by tough new restrictions on energy use" called for by the Kyoto treaty.

If ratified, the treaty would require reductions in carbon dioxin emissions from burning fossil fuels.

A video is shown. And then the leaders of the Black and Hispanic groups present lay out the chief findings of the study—that America's minority community would be hardest hit by a recession triggered by the Kyoto treaty, that the treaty would put more than one million Black and Hispanic worker jobs at risk, that higher unemployment, reduced earning power, and higher prices for energy and other consumer goods would push millions of people of color into poverty.

So, now we're almost an hour into the press conference, and not one mention is made of the coal industry's involvement with the study—a salient factoid if there ever was one in the context of this press conference.

We're sitting in the press area, and next to us is sitting Stephen Miller, the president of CEED, the coal front group. So, we point out that CEED is a corporate front group. And we wanted to know—did the coal industry pay for this report?

Yes, the coal industry paid $40,000 for the report, Miller admits.

And Harry Alford, of the National Black Chamber of Commerce, said that his organization has received checks from Texaco and General Motors and others, but "that money has nothing to do with what we are doing here today."

"I take offense at your thinking that our groups are here because someone gave us a check to say something," Alford said. "So, I'm a little insulted. And I do think the question is racial."

Lionel Hurst appeared insulted, too. By Alford. Hurst is the Ambassador to the United States from Antigua and Barbuda. Tipped off to the press conference, Hurst attended and confronted Alford. He pointed out that people of color communities around the world are already suffering unduly from the impacts of global warming. "Failure to act internationally on global warming will pose the greatest costs to the most vulnerable nations of the world due to sea level rise and the spread of infectious diseases in a warmer world," Hurst said.

Also offended were the African-American activists who for years have been working on the question of polluting industries dumping on minority communities.

These activists, including Dr. Joseph Lowrey of the Southern Christian Leadership Conference, and Connie Tucker of the Southern Organizing Committee, sent a letter to all members of Congress, pointing out that the risks to minority communities from global warming "are much greater than the dangers from the Kyoto Protocol that appear in the biased predictions of the coal lobby."

In the letter, the activists pointed out that asthma death rates are two times higher for Blacks than for Whites and that a recent national assessment of the regional impacts of global warming on the United States found that higher temperatures, coupled with air pollution in minority neighborhoods, would further aggravate asthma problems. And the coal industry study ignored the substantial long-term economic benefits of mitigating global warming.

These arguments didn't faze Oscar Sanchez, executive director of the Labor Council for Latin American Advancement, which represents 1.5 million Hispanic members of the AFL-CIO.

He defended his group's participation in the coal industry-funded event and laid down a slippery slope philosophy familiar to public interest groups throughout the city co-opted by big business money.

"We had a story to tell and we found a way of doing it," Sanchez told reporters during the press conference. "We found a sponsor. It's not uncommon. It's not like it's something that never happened before."

National Breast Cancer Industry Month

October 26, 2000

If Hallmark can make Mother's Day, Father's Day and National Secretary's Week into national holidays, why not other companies?

Perhaps that was going through the mind of executives at AstraZeneca, the drug manufacturer, when they decided to invent National Breast Cancer Awareness Month.

This October has been the fifteenth annual National Breast Cancer Awareness Month, and the event is gaining an ever-higher profile. It garners abundant media attention, and is a growing favorite for corporate charitable work. Ms. PacMan, the first official spokesperson for the National Association of Breast Cancer Organizations (NABCO), is working to promote breast health throughout October. Georgette Klinger, a cosmetics company, is donating a portion of its October revenues to NABCO. Hickory Farms has produced a National Breast Cancer Awareness Month gift basket, the Gift of Hope, that includes breast cancer educational information. Loehmann's, the fashion retailer, hosted special shopping nights at its Manhattan and Beverly Hills stores, donating a portion of proceeds to NABCO. Bristol-Myers Squibb and the California-based Longs Drug Stores are donating a portion of their October sales of select products to NABCO. American Express is encouraging people to Shop for a Cure in September and October, when certain AmEx purchases will trigger a corporate donation to breast cancer research.

National Breast Cancer Awareness Month's core message is the importance of early detection, with a special emphasis on regular mammography exams.

So lots of organizations, media outlets and companies join together to deliver a health promotion message. Who could object?

Barbara Brenner, for one. Brenner is executive director of Breast Cancer Action, a hard-hitting grassroots organization based in San Francisco.

"Because of Breast Cancer Awareness Month, everybody thinks wearing a pink ribbon and racing for the cure will solve the problem," she says.

The soft sell approach, combined with the exclusive focus on early detection, keeps people from understanding "what is really going on," she says. On the one hand, while women who detect breast cancer early are better off than those who detect it late, Brenner says, early detection is certainly no guarantee. On the other hand, the focus on detection comes at the expense of any critical questioning about causation and intelligent approaches to seeking a cure.

A dramatically different approach is called for, Brenner says.

First, cancer prevention efforts must embrace the precautionary principle—the idea that when an activity raises threats of harm to human health or the environment, precautionary measures should be taken in the absence of scientific certainty. As part of the Bay Area Toxics Link Coalition, Breast Cancer Action is pushing a Stop Cancer Where It Starts initiative that has succeeded in getting San Francisco, Oakland and Berkeley to incorporate the precautionary principle in local regulations.

Second, Brenner says, the cancer research agenda should be restructured. Breast Cancer Action is calling for a national Rachel Carson Project to fund a half dozen multi-disciplinary cancer research centers that would focus on finding more effective and less toxic cancer treatments, and on researching cancer causes. A key element of the plan: products invented by the centers cannot be patented.

This is not exactly the agenda of the cancer establishment, which is hostile to the idea that environmental causation is a significant part of the story of the rising incidence of breast cancer in the United States.

And by now, National Breast Cancer Awareness Month is both a creature of the entire cancer establishment and a reflection of its ideology. As Kathy Paranzino, program manager at AstraZeneca says, National Breast Cancer Awareness Month "has taken on a life of its own."

Founded by Zeneca, then a subsidiary of Imperial Chemical Industries (ICI), a giant chemical firm, along with the American Academy of Family Physicians and Cancer Care Inc., National Breast Cancer Awareness Month is now governed by a 17 organization board that includes the American Cancer Society, the Centers for Disease Control, the National Cancer Institute and the Susan G. Komen Breast Cancer Foundation. All funding for the official activities comes from the AstraZeneca Healthcare Foundation, though board members offer in-kind support and countless organizations conduct their own activities during the month.

AstraZeneca, no longer connected to ICI, now has no direct corporate interest in turning attention away from potential links between pesticides, chemical pollution and breast cancer. But as maker of tamoxifen, the controversial drug that has been approved to reduce the risk of contracting cancer in women with a high risk of breast cancer, it remains highly desirable for the company to be associated in the public mind with efforts to address breast cancer.

Other corporate members of the cancer establishment— such as General Electric, the heavily advertised maker of mammography machines and also a major industrial polluter—have a more direct interest in turning companies away from potential environmental causes of cancer.

The prospect of companies from Bristol Myers Squibb to American Express rallying in support of Stop Cancer Where It Starts month seems slight. Instead, this effort will be carried forward by an energetic, grassroots environmental health movement.

Busted: the Genentech/American Heart Association Connection

November 10, 2000

For years, Genentech Inc.'s clotbuster drug tPA has been used to treat heart attacks.

Last year, the American Heart Association published guidelines for physicians advising that tPA be used to treat strokes.

Whether these new guidelines will help stroke patients or not is an open question. Whether it helps Genentech's bottom line is decided—it will.

Dr. Jerome Hoffman, professor of medicine at the UCLA Medical School, sat on the American Heart Association panel that hashed out the new guidelines. He was the only member of the panel who raised serious questions about recommending using tPA to treat strokes.

Dr. Hoffman says there is clear-cut evidence that clotbusters are helpful in treating heart attack patients.

But when it comes to treating stroke, there is a great deal of controversy. While clotbuster drugs do some good in treating stroke, they also can cause bleeding in the brain.

"The Food and Drug Administration approved this drug to treat stroke on the basis of a single study by the National Institutes of Health, which I find worrisome," Dr. Hoffman said. "The study shows a marginal benefit in a very small number of stroke patients. Furthermore, I believe that study conflicts with evidence from some other studies that show increased risks with use of these drugs."

In the previous version of its guidelines, the American Heart Association recommended using clotbusters for stroke. "But they gave it a guarded recommendation," Dr. Hoffman told us. "Last fall they were reconsidering it. And a proposal had been made to upgrade it to a class one recommendation—slam dunk—definitely use it."

The American Heart Association calls itself "the largest voluntary health organization dedicated to fighting heart disease and stroke."

According to the group's 1999 annual report, it has received $1 million or more from some of the nation's largest pharmaceutical companies, including Bristol-Myers Squibb, Hoechst Marion Roussel, Novartis, Pfizer, AstraZeneca, SmithKline Beecham—and Genentech.

Curious to find out more details, we called on the Association acting science chief Dr. Rodman Starke.

Dr. Starke said that over the past 10 years, Genentech had given more than $10 million to the American Heart Association, including $2 million to build the Association's conference center in Dallas, Texas, making it one of the group's top corporate donors.

Did Genentech get anything in return for building the conference center?

"We put up a plaque inside the conference center thanking Genentech for its contribution and have allowed the company to hold a meeting of its sales reps at the conference center," Dr. Starke said.

We questioned whether Genentech's largesse created an environment conducive to the writing of guidelines calling on physicians to treat stroke with Genentech's tPA—over the informed objections of one of the panelists—Dr. Hoffman.

"Poppycock," Dr. Starke says. "There is no influence of any corporate supporters of what the guidelines are going to say. The guidelines wouldn't be any good if people would point to them and say—well, these were bought."

We asked Dr. Hoffman whether he believed that the Genentech money influenced the American Heart Association on tPA.

"I don't have reason to believe that there is a quid pro quo with anyone in the American Heart Association," he said. "On the other hand, many of the volunteers on the panel have worked for drug companies, and while people who do research for drug companies often deny that this has any affect on their science, studies show it does have an effect—results tend to be better for proprietary research than for non-proprietary research."

Dr. Starke said he would get us the conflict information on the people who developed and wrote the guidelines for treating stroke. But then an American Heart Association spokesperson called us to say that the conflict reports were "confidential," and that we couldn't have them. Instead, he would set us up with a Mary Fran Hazinski, a co-editor of the guidelines. She would give us what we needed to know about possible conflicts.

Hazinski said she wanted us to know that the guidelines went through 10 or 11 layers at the American Heart Association before being released.

She said that she didn't have access to the conflict statements for all of the people involved in the process, but that she recalled that one or two of the panelists may have received a grant from Genentech.

She wasn't sure, she said, whether the people involved in the process were required to disclose any and all money—speaking fees, for example—received from Genentech. She said she didn't even know about Genentech's $10 million in contributions to the American Heart Association—until we told her—and she was writing and editing the guidelines recommending tPA for stroke.

"I think it is wonderful that I never knew about the Genentech funding," Hazinski said. "Clearly it could not have influenced me if I didn't know about it."

Anyone who knows a young doctor knows that they are showered with gifts, and trips and speaking invitations from drug companies. Drug company largesse knows no bounds.

Most doctors express astonishment that anyone would think that these gifts and trips would affect their behavior. But as Dr. Hoffman points out, there is a large literature documenting the many ways that it does in fact affect physician behavior.

"Of course it affects physician behavior," he says.

That's why he refuses to take anything—a canvas bag, a notepad, a trip to the Bahamas, or a speaking fee—from drug companies.

And so should the American Heart Association, no matter how sweet the corporate candycane.

PART SIX

LABOR

Corporate America has never had any illusions about the nature of class conflict. It is real, heated and ongoing, business leaders know, the wonders of the New Economy notwithstanding.

For most of the last decades, business has had labor on the run. Increased capital mobility and foreign competition, widespread corporate downsizing, a politically weak labor movement, unenforced labor laws and technological innovation have all combined to strengthen business power. Employers have used their power to intimidate and threaten workers, so that they fear unionizing, asking for a raise or even quitting and looking for another job. A ruthless employer class blends these multiple sources of job insecurity into a whole greater than the parts. Employers use threats of plant relocation to bust unions. They rely on weak or non-existent unions to permit downsizing. They capitalize on technological changes to speed restructuring and to shift production abroad.

The right to join a union in the United States is mocked by massive employer lawbreaking in unionization drives. One in ten union supporters campaigning to form a union is fired, illegally. Employers routinely threaten, illegally, to close their facilities if workers elect to form a union.

Similar tactics and power plays are evident in collective bargaining, with the threat to shift production overseas a specter looming over negotiations in the manufacturing sector.

On the shop floor, employers tolerate preventable workplace hazards because enforcement of occupational safety and health laws is so weak, the underlying laws and regulations are flawed and even those workers who do have a union generally do not have enough power to demand preventive action. As a result, in the United States alone, 6,000 workers die each year from workplace trauma, and another 50,000 to 60,000 die every year, at minimum, from occupational disease. Millions of workers each year suffer from workplace injuries, leaving many victims with aching backs, bad knees, amputated fingers or other pains and disabilities that diminish quality of life for months, years or often a lifetime.

What's Black and White and Red All Over?

March 9, 1999

Let's say you are a newspaper boy, or girl.

And you are riding your bicycle up and down the street delivering newspapers.

And a car runs hits your bike, you fall and suffer severe injuries.

Who pays your medical bill?

Well, most likely, you are not covered under your state's workers' compensation law, even though you are a worker.

This is a real issue for the hundreds of thousands newspaper carriers, the vast majority of whom are young teenagers.

Between 1992 and 1997, 99 news vendors were killed on the job, eleven of them under the age of 18. A 1994 Newspaper Association of America survey found there were about 450,000 child and adult carriers in the United States and that only 5.9 percent of carriers were covered by workers' compensation.

The reason newspaper carriers are not covered by workers' comp is simple enough: in a decades-long campaign, the newspaper industry has successfully sought to exclude newspaper carriers from workers' comp laws, minimum wage laws, workers' safety laws, right up to and including social security laws. They have done this by pressuring legislatures to write newspaper carriers out of these laws designed to protect workers.

Earlier this year, the newspaper industry's dirty little secret was exposed by University of Iowa Professor Marc Linder. ["What's Black and White and Red All Over? The Blood Tax On Newspapers—or, How Publishers Exclude Newscarriers from Workers' Compensation," (3 *Loyola Poverty Law Journal* 57 August 1998)].

Linder sent this law review article to reporters and columnists around the country—reporters who had covered his research in the past.

But on this very hot labor issue dear to the hearts of newspaper industry, Linder was given the cold shoulder.

"I have been told directly by various reporters and columnists that they would never get it past their editors and they
don't want to waste their journalistic, political capital on this
matter because it is not going to get published anyway and they
don't want to struggle with their editors over it," Linder told us
recently.

One reporter proved the exception: Associated Press
workplace reporter Maggie Jackson. Last year, Jackson had written about Linder's pathbreaking study about how corporations
were infringing on basic worker rights, such as the right to use
the bathroom. [*Void Where Prohibited: Rest Breaks and the Right
to Urinate on Company Time*, by Marc Linder and Ingrid
Nygaard, (Cornell University Press, 1998)]. Jackson's story on
the right to urinate went out on the AP wire and was published
in newspapers around the world.

Jackson interviewed Linder and others about the newspaper delivery-workers' comp issue, and wrote the story. She
assumed that her bosses at the Associated Press, a cooperative
of newspaper companies, would run it.

Instead, in a brazen act of censorship, her bosses killed it.

Jackson confirmed to us that the story was "spiked," as she
put it, but she would not answer questions as to why.

Linder too does not know why.

"I can only speculate that either the people who killed it
have so internalized the thought patterns of the publishers who
cooperatively own the AP that they know on their own that
this is not a subject that would redound to the benefit of the
cooperative owners," Linder said. "Or someone from the publishers' side caught wind of the story, called them and killed it.
This latter point is total speculation on my part. I don't know
that, but I can imagine it."

When asked about the workers' comp problem, newspaper
industry executives argue that since carriers are independent

contractors and not employees, the carriers must assume the risks.

"Almost uniformly, their response was mechanical—the children are independent contractors and not our problem," Linder said. "This is the mantra the newspapers have been chanting for decades."

In his research, Linder found that some newspaper executives understand the problem and want to do something about it.

"I know that the managers of the *St. Petersburg Times* say that they treat all of their delivery people as employees and they cover them with workers' compensation," Linder said. "The circulation manager at the *Columbus Dispatch* is very concerned about the children and he personally got the owner of the newspaper to treat all of the children as employees and to cover them with workers' compensation. The *Dispatch* is independently owned and that is one reason they are able to do it."

Industry executives ought to do the right thing and follow the lead of their brethren at the Columbus and St. Petersburg papers and attack this problem head on. It can't cost them all that much money to fold their child laborers into workers' comp programs. And with the ever-expanding news outlets on the internet, they can't expect to bury this story for long.

GE: Every Plant on a Barge

May 17, 2000

There is probably no more "American" corporation than General Electric—and no company with more of an anational world outlook than GE.

And no company's record better illustrates the glories of corporate globalization for the well-off, and the misery for the many.

Founded by the American icon Thomas Edison, GE is now headed by Jack Welch, who has said, "Ideally you'd have every plant you own on a barge"—ready to move if any national government tried to impose restraints on the factories' operations, or if workers demanded better wages and working conditions.

While Welch's 20-year reign has been a golden era for shareholders—the company's stock value has risen three times more than the Dow average, leading *Forbes* magazine to name Welch the "Most Admired CEO of the Century"—it has been a disaster for employees.

GE has slashed its U.S. workforce by almost half since 1986. The numbers are down "because of speed up, downsizing, outsourcing, plant closings, you name it," says Chris Townsend, political director of the United Electrical (UE) workers.

GE has globalized its operations by shifting production to low-wage countries. (And even in these countries, the jobs remain precarious: GE recently shuttered a factory in Turkey to move it to lower-wage Hungary—and it has threatened to close a factory in Hungary and move it to India. Union officials in Malaysia say they fear GE "putting our plant on a barge and moving to Vietnam," according to InterPress Service.)

Now GE appears no longer satisfied to close its own plants—it wants to shut down those of suppliers, too. In a startling memo obtained by *Business Week*, GE Aircraft Engines (GEAE)—a hugely profitable division—told suppliers that they would have to move to Mexico if they hoped to continue their relationship with GE. GEAE has held what it calls "supplier migration" conferences in Cincinnati, near its headquarters, and in Monterrey, where an aerospace industrial park is being built.

An internal report on a GEAE meeting with its suppliers says, "GE set the tone early and succinctly: 'Migrate or be out of business; not a matter of if, just when. This is not a seminar to provide you information. We expect you to move and move quickly.'"

These kinds of tactics obviously leave GE's workers (not to mention those in supplier plants) in a weak negotiating position.

New contract negotiations between GE and its unionized workforce in the United States are set to begin later this month, with GE's collective bargaining agreements expiring at the end of June.

In an unusual arrangement that has its origins in the anti-communism that wreaked the labor movement especially following World War II, 14 U.S. unions represent GE workers. Although the unions, including the two unions with national contracts—the International Union of Electronic workers (IUE) and the progressive UE—now work relatively well together, the balkanized representation system further weakens labor negotiators.

In preparation for this year's negotiations, the GE Coordinated Bargaining Committee, which includes the 14 unions, has undertaken a corporate campaign. They've high-lighted egregious GE practices and generated public support and sympathy. In one sign that they do have some power, efforts to publicize GE's use of pension funds as an accounting profit center (because the $50 billion pension pool is overfunded by $25 billion, GE is able to claim investment gains on the pension funds as paper profits) have resulted in GE agreeing to provide expanded pension benefits.

GE workers have also taken the first steps to deal with the

globalization of the company. In March, the International Metalworkers Federation held a meeting in Washington, D.C. to bring together GE union representatives from 20 countries. While they are certainly a long way from global bargaining with the company—with some progressive unionists cautioning that global bargaining may not even be desirable—they did agree to meaningful information exchanges and solidarity activities.

Meanwhile, the tiny UE has done more impressive and far-reaching solidarity work than any other U.S. union, maintaining a long-time partnership with the FAT labor federation in Mexico, the organization of authentic Mexican unions.

But addressing the problem of runaway GE will require more than international union solidarity, as crucial as it is. A far stronger and aggressive labor movement might be able to stop plant closings and job exports through direct action and collective bargaining, or it might be able to win national legislation or even international trade rules to block GE and other companies from employing a "factory barge" strategy.

For now, however, GE appears relatively free to trumpet its American heritage while betraying the U.S. workers who built the company ... and turning its back on its new workers outside of the United States if still greater profits are to be found elsewhere.

Business Power and Mobility

November 29, 2000

The election season makes it patently clear how Big Business is able to transform its financial resources into political power via campaign contributions.

But an even more fundamental source of business power is corporations' control over investment decisions, and the tax, trade and investment rules which enhance capital mobility. The ability to shift production to different locations, or threaten to shift production, gives corporations enormous leverage over the political process and over workers.

Want to adopt serious environmental standards to stem the corporate poisoning of the air, water and land? Get ready to face the threat of plant closures and job shifting. Want to force companies to bear a reasonable share of the tax burden? Be prepared to face company moves to lower tax havens. Want to mandate payment of a living wage to all workers? Plan to hear how business will be forced to move to Mexico or China.

Nowhere is the raw power connected to corporate mobility more apparent than in labor-management relations, as Kate Bronfenbrenner, director of labor education research at Cornell's School of Industrial and Labor Relations, makes clear in a new paper, "Uneasy Terrain" (see http://www.ustdrc.gov/research/bronfenbrenner.pdf).

When faced with union organizing campaigns, employers routinely threaten to close their plant and move elsewhere. Understandably, these threats intimidate workers—a union won't do you any good if you don't have a job—and they are tremendously successful at defeating union organizing drives.

In the most comprehensive survey ever of U.S. union organizing campaigns, Bronfenbrenner found that "the majority of employers consistently, pervasively and extremely effectively tell workers either directly or indirectly that if they ask for too much, or don't give concessions, or try to organize, strike or fight for good jobs with good benefits, the company will close, move out of state or move across the border, just as so many other plants have done before."

In union organizing drives in the United States in 1998 and 1998, she found, more than half of all employers threatened to close all or part of the facility if workers voted to join a union.

But the situation is even worse than that figure suggests, because for some types employers it is difficult to make credible threats to move—hotels and hospitals, for example, are to a considerable extent tied to place.

In mobile industries—manufacturing and other companies that can credibly threaten to shift production—the plant closing threat rate was 68 percent. In all manufacturing, it was 71 percent. In food processing, it was 71 percent.

These numbers mark a worrisome upturn from a previous Bronfenbrenner survey, undertaken for the Labor Secretariat of the Commission for Labor Cooperation and published in 1997. Bronfenbrenner's data from 1993-1995 showed a threat rate of 64 percent among manufacturers, 21 percent among food processors.

(That earlier study, prepared for a commission created by one of the NAFTA side agreements, was suppressed by the Clinton administration. Eventually liberated, it provided some of the key evidence leading to the defeat of fast track.)

Employers deliver the threats directly (after posting pictures of shut down facilities, supervisors asked workers at a Mitsubishi plant in Tennessee, "Is your family ready to move to Mexico?") or more indirectly. For multinationals, Bronfenbrenner told us, there is a pervasive "silent threat. ... The map on the wall" showing the locations of a company around the world is an ongoing reminder that the company can easily do business elsewhere.

Employers know the threats work, Bronfenbrenner says. Anti-union training materials emphasize that "fear is the most effective tool," she explains.

And the evidence backs up the commonsense insight that threats to close effectively intimidate workers.

"Union election win rates were significantly lower in units where plant closing threats occurred (38 percent) than in units without plant closing threats (51 percent)," Bronfenbrenner found. "Win rates were especially low (24 percent) in those campaigns where employers made specific threats to move to another country. Win rates were also significantly lower in mobile industries where the threat of closure was more credible."

Unions can overcome plant-closing threats, Bronfenbrenner says, by running aggressive campaigns that involve rank-and-file union members as organizers and actively involve and energize the workers who are being organized. But the challenge is immense, especially given the array of other anti-union tactics, including firing of union supporters, that corporations regularly employ.

Dealing with the problem of plant-closing threats, at least in the union organizing context, will require two major reforms, Bronfenbrenner concludes. First, labor law must more clearly delineate such threats as illegal, and impose big enough penalties to deter employers from making them. Second, trade, investment and tax policy must be changed to limit corporate mobility, and to block employers from shifting operations to avoid unionization.

That's not just a pro-union agenda. It is a basic pro-democracy one.

Marc Rich's Hidden History as a Union-Buster

February 12, 2001

Longtime fugitive from justice Marc Rich has become the most notorious recipient of a presidential pardon since Richard Nixon. President Clinton issued a pardon for the commodities trader in the final hours of his tenure in office.

What is now widely known about Rich has cast a dark cloud over what Clinton hoped would be a glorious exit from the presidency. Charged with income tax fraud and conspiracy, Rich fled to Switzerland, from which he could not be extradited. Living in the lap of luxury, he continued his wheeling and dealing in international commodities markets, including through trades with apartheid South Africa. He invested heavily in seeking a pardon, courting the Israeli government (dethroned Israel President Ehud Barak personally lobbied Clinton for Rich's pardon), hiring top-ranking officials from Democratic and Republican administrations to represent him, and relying on his ex-wife to lavish money on Democrats during the Clinton years.

What is not widely known, at least outside of West Virginia and certain labor circles, is that Rich played a central role in one of the highest profile union-busting efforts the United States has seen in recent decades.

In the early 1990s, Marc Rich was the power-behind-the-scenes at the Ravenswood Aluminum Corporation (RAC) facility in Ravenswood, West Virginia, site of one of the most embittered U.S. labor-management disputes of recent decades.

The Ravenswood conflict has been chronicled by Tom Juravich and Kate Bronfenbrenner in their inspiring account, *Ravenswood: The Steelworkers' Victory and the Revival of American Labor* (Ithaca, New York: ILR/Cornell University Press, 1999).

In 1990, in a premeditated effort to break the union, RAC

locked out its 1,700 workers, members of the United Steelworkers of America, and hired permanent replacements.

As the contract deadline neared, RAC installed surveillance cameras, new security systems and a chainlink fence around the perimeter of the facility. The night of the lockout, the company brought in a goon squad security force equipped with riot gear, clubs, tear gas and video cameras used to constantly monitor the workers' pickets. The goons introduced a climate of fear and made violence on the picket lines, and in the town, an ever-present fear.

Caught unprepared, the Steelworkers' local was able to keep all but a handful of workers from crossing the picket line and union solidarity was strong and militant, but RAC was ready to wait the workers out.

As the lockout progressed, the Steelworkers' international union became engaged, and eventually launched a corporate campaign to complement the local's efforts. That corporate campaign took them to Marc Rich.

The Ravenswood plant, which had been owned by Kaiser Aluminum for four decades, passed into the ownership of RAC in 1988. The union discovered that, behind a convoluted corporate ownership smokescreen, stood one man with a controlling interest in RAC: Marc Rich.

It is unlikely that Rich initially knew what RAC was up to when the lockout began—RAC was just a piece in his global corporate puzzle. But about four months into the conflict, the union had made the Rich connection and was calling on him to end the lockout.

"From that point on, Rich was culpable for what went on and the suffering the Ravenswood workers went through," says Bronfenbrenner.

For 20 long months, the workers lived on minimal strike benefits, six months worth of unemployment benefits and donated food and supplies. Being out of work for so long, even from a lockout where union solidarity remains high, takes an emotional toll to match the financial one. It is no exaggeration when Bronfenbrenner speaks of the suffering of the workers and their families.

As the Steelworkers tracked Rich to Switzerland and began applying pressure on his business operations in Europe, the corporate campaign moved to a new plane and the union discovered how extensive was Rich's reach.

Soon they found themselves negotiating with Leonard Garment, White House Counsel under Richard Nixon, and William Bradford Reynolds, the number two at the Reagan Justice Department. Both Garment and Reynolds worked for Rich—who would later show that he was right to trust in high-priced, politically connected legal help when Jack Quinn, former Clinton White House Counsel, would do the crucial work to win Rich his pardon.

As the Steelworkers' campaign got closer to Rich's significant financial interests, union representatives received numerous death threats.

When left-leaning Michael Manley was elected president of Jamaica in 1989, the Steelworkers were hopeful he would follow through on promises to cut his predecessor's close ties to Rich—ties which gave Rich access to Jamaica's alumina at less than half the market rate. But when Manley faced immediate pressure from the International Monetary Fund to raise foreign capital, Rich gave the government a $50 million cash advance. Manley then backed down from efforts to end the Rich connection.

But the Steelworkers' comprehensive international campaign did achieve major successes, including blocking Rich's purchase of the Slovakian National Aluminum Company and a majority stake in a luxury Romanian hotel, convincing Budweiser and Stroh's not to buy RAC aluminum, and heaping unwanted publicity on Rich. Meanwhile, local solidarity remained strong.

This all cost Rich. In April 1992, Rich finally moved to

replace management at RAC and end the lockout. The final contract terms were not entirely favorable to the workers, but they had at least succeeded in defeating the company's vicious attempt to bust the union.

Asked about Clinton's pardon of Rich, Dan Stidham, who was president of the Ravenswood local during the strike and is now retired, says it is "really disappointing."

Stidham modestly says that he's "pretty upset that Clinton would pardon that guy after all we went through for 20 months."

In granting the pardon, Clinton probably did not know of Rich's odious role in the Ravenswood lockout. Perhaps, as he claims, he did not know of Rich's ex-wife's support for the Democrats.

But neither of those facts, if they are facts, makes the pardon smell any better.

If Clinton didn't know, he should have. And if he didn't know, it only highlights how in an increasingly corrupt political system, money not only can gain you access to the highest levels of influence and but can enable corporate lawbreakers to launder their image and reputations.

Ironically, even though Rich has won the right to return to the United States without facing trial, the attention surrounding the pardon has permanently stained his reputation.

That may be some small solace to the workers at Ravenswood, who will forever know Rich as a criminal in more ways than one.

Time to Permanently Replace
Weak Labor Law

April 18, 2001

The recent Cincinnati riots are a jarring reminder to white people in the United States, and anyone else who needs reminding, that the basic civil rights of racial minorities are all too regularly violated in a country that fancies itself the land of the free.

Maybe it's time for working people of all races to undertake a similarly eye-opening, nonviolent insurrection to remind the country how routinely another set of civil rights—workers' rights to organize and collectively bargain—are trampled.

In U.S. union organizing contests, employers illegally fire an estimated one in ten union supporters. In half of all organizing drives, employers threaten to shut down or move operations. Among the most powerful of all coercive techniques, employer threats to close are illegal, but may be issued in a way that makes them technically legal.

Employers resist unionization through a wide array of anti-union tactics, legal and illegal, and all designed to interfere with workers' right to self-organize. These tactics range from captive meetings where employers or their consultants deliver anti-union jeremiads to their employees, to surveillance, to bribes or special favors to employees who oppose the union. Kate Bronfenbrenner of Cornell University, the leading U.S. researcher of union organizing practices and employer responses, finds that more than 60 percent of employers confronting a union organizing drive use five or more anti-union tactics.

When workers do succeed in organizing, they often confront employers who simply refuse to bargain. Less than half of new unions are successfully able to win a first contract.

Even the rights of workers with well-established unions are violated. Most importantly, unionized workers' most powerful bargaining tool, the right to strike, is effectively neutered by a preposterous Supreme Court doctrine which holds that while workers cannot be fired for exercising their right to strike, they can be "permanently replaced." There are some slight differences between being fired and permanently replaced, but none so consequential as to make a difference to workers considering striking. In the last two decades, employers have become increasingly willing to permanently replace striking workers—with the result that strikes are at record lows.

One man who explicitly makes the links between civil rights and labor rights is William Gould, who from 1993 to 1998 was the chair of the National Labor Relations Board—the body which adjudicates allegations of labor law violations. Gould views the 1935 National Labor Relations Act as continuing the mission of the Thirteenth Amendment, adopted in the wake of the Civil War, of making labor free.

If basic worker rights are to be respected in the United States, Gould says, labor law needs to be revitalized to provide meaningful protections to workers.

"It makes a mockery of the law to say as we do that the law protects the right to strike," he points out, "and yet simultaneously say that for all practical purposes you can lose your job as a result of the strike."

"The remedies at the disposal of the Board are extremely limited," Gould told us. "All too frequently the remedies are a license fee for illegal behavior." The penalty for illegal firings, for example, is payment of back pay minus what the fired worker earned between the firing and issuance of judgment.

Having witnessed the widespread abuse of worker rights as head of the agency charged with protecting those rights, Gould stands by the reform proposals he put forward in a 1993 book, Agenda for Reform. We don't agree with all of Gould's reform agenda—notably, his support for certain kinds of labor-management cooperation and some limits on union action—but many of his proposals are essential if workers' basic rights are to be vindicated.

Among the changes in labor law Gould says should be enacted:

- Treble damages for illegal firings and egregious misconduct by employers;
- Mandated access for unions to employees they are seeking to organize, through presence on plant property and access to names and addresses of employees at an early stage in the organizing campaign;
- The recognition of unions that sign up a majority of a workplace's employees ("card check") or snap elections upon union request;
- Mandatory arbitration of first contracts, where union and employer are unable to arrive at an initial collective bargaining agreement; and
- Repeal of the absurd permanent replacement doctrine, to give life to the right to strike.

Unfortunately, there is a paucity of instances in U.S. history where documented need has been sufficient to spur the creation or full enforcement of fundamental civil rights. Such changes rarely emerge from anything but sustained social protest and disruption of business as usual.

PART SEVEN

THE INSANITY DEFENSE

9-11 changed the face of U.S., and world, politics. In summer 2001, the Bush administration was on the rocks, its popularity plummeting, and opposition growing increasingly emboldened.

Then, with the tragedy of the attacks on the World Trade Center and the Pentagon, the Bush presidency was transformed.

Even before the advent of the Bush administration and before the tragedy of September 11, 2001, the military-industrial complex had thrown down the gauntlet. It was time for defense spending, which had remained roughly flat since the end of the Cold War, to escalate. A compliant Clinton administration agreed, and began the process of boosting the military budget.

Then came 9-11. The Bush administration and most of the nation's political leadership amd media elite unified around the notion that the best response to violence was more violence. The U.S. intention in Afghanistan wasn't to kill civilians, but at least as many civilians died in the U.S. military action against the Taliban as in the al-Qaeda attack on the World Trade Center and Pentagon.

For the Bush administration, 9-11 was a political savior. A population that in summer 2001 was growing increasingly disenchanted with a president they did not elect in the first place suddenly warmed to George W. Bush. After 9-11, Bush's popularity soared.

Eventually, though, that bump in the polls wore off. With the November 2002 mid-term elections approaching, the administration decided that a manufactured crisis in Iraq would catapult Republicans to electoral success. Assisted by a stunningly incompetent Democratic Party, the ploy worked.

But there was more than electoral gamesmanship going on. Geopolitical concerns about controlling oil, a cabal of Bush insiders who wanted to assert U.S. authority to use violence without restraint, and the President's desire to finish the war his father started, among other factors, drove the United States to war.

Retrospectively, it is obvious that the war was groundless. But it was obvious prospectively, too, to anyone who cared to know. Most of the Democratic Party leadership and the hawkish media were among those who did not care to know.

The results have been disastrous. Thousands of Iraqis have been killed and the country thrown into chaos. Hundreds of U.S. soldiers have lost their lives, the vast majority after George Bush declared "Mission Accomplished." Tens of billions of dollars have been wasted on military operations, with the bill set to rise for the indefinite future. There are more rather than fewer terrorists in the world. The risk of weapons of mass destruction being used against the United States has worsened, as U.S. occupiers have failed to keep close watch over Iraq's nuclear materials. And a dangerous precedent has been set, enabling almost any military force to point to the U.S. doctrine of preventive war to rationalize their own actions.

The Insanity Defense

January 18, 1999

Need a definition for Washington?

Try institutional insanity.

Consider this: The United States, the world's only remaining military superpower, is about to embark on a military buildup unmatched since the peak of the Reagan-era Cold War.

President Clinton is preparing to propose a boost in the defense budget of $112 billion over six years—on top of the already monstrous $265 billion of federal money spent annually on the military. The weapons procurement budget alone is scheduled to grow 50 percent in the next half decade. And the Congressional Republicans are set to demand an even greater jump in military spending.

What's happened, you might ask: Was there a coup in Russia? Has the Cold War resumed?

Uh, no. It is not the Empire that's struck again, it's the military-industrial complex.

During the Clinton presidency, the U.S. defense industry—with encouragement and subsidies from the Pentagon—has undergone an ear-splitting consolidation that has left but three major contractors: Lockheed Martin, Boeing and Raytheon. Today's Lockheed Martin is the product of the merger of Lockheed, Martin Marietta, Loral and parts of General Dynamics. Boeing leaped to the top tier of the contractor pack with its acquisition of McDonnell Douglas. Raytheon gobbled up Hughes.

With manufacturing facilities spread across the United States, these three companies now have enormous political influence—they can promise that new military contracts will mean jobs in the districts of hundreds of members of Congress, and in nearly every state. They supplement this structural power with huge campaign contributions—more than $8.5 million in the 1997-1998 electoral cycle, according to the Center for Responsive politics—and even bigger lobbying investments—

nearly $50 million in 1997 alone, according to the Center. To complete the package, the industry invests in a variety of hawkish policy institutes and front groups, all of which churn reports, issue alerts, factsheets, congressional testimony and op-eds on the critical need for more, and more, and more defense spending.

Combined with the powerful lobby from the Pentagon and its chicken-little worries about shortcomings in U.S. military "readiness" and the ability of the United States to fight two major wars simultaneously, the defense contractors have successfully positioned themselves to reap the benefits of a new explosion in military spending.

As William Hartung of the World Policy Institute notes in a new report, "Military Industrial Complex Revisited," nothing indicates the power of the contractor lobby more than its ability to extract more money from Congress for weapons purchases than the Pentagon itself has requested.

Hartung highlights the example of the C-130 transport plane, which is made by Lockheed Martin just outside of the congressional district of former Speaker of the House Newt Gingrich. In the last 20 years, the U.S. Air Force has asked for five C-130s, but Congress has funded 256. "This ratio of 50 planes purchased for every one requested by the Pentagon may well be a record in the annals of pork barrel politics," Hartung writes. The C-130s go for about $75 million a piece.

Even more remarkable, perhaps, is the "Star Wars" program. With the collapse of the Soviet Union, the program's original mission no longer exists. Although the Pentagon has poured $55 billion into the program in a decade and a half, as Hartung notes, it has been a miserable failure in technical terms. Undeterred, the Congressional leadership added an extra $1 billion in Star Wars funding in the 1999 federal budget. Chalk up another victory for Lockheed and Boeing.

But nothing compares to bonanza that the defense sector is about to reap. Without even the bogeyman of a perceived

Soviet threat and in a time of rigid adherence to budget auster-
ity, the weapons makers and their allies are about to usher in a
new era of military profligacy and industrial waste.

With the U.S. infrastructure crumbling, its Medicare system imperiled, child poverty at unconscionable levels in a time
of unparalleled economic expansion and global warming threatening the well-being of the entire planet, a remotely sensible
version of "national security" would prioritize these concerns
over maintaining the military budget at current levels, let alone
increasing it.

Unfortunately, the lobbies for public works, the sick and
aged, the poor and the environment cannot match the influence of the weapons makers. Their urgings that the federal government invest to address real problems that trouble the entire
society, or at least large segments of it, are dismissed as "unreasonable."

In Washington, where things are upside down, it is the
madmen in the Pentagon and at Lockheed Martin who are considered reasonable.

Respond to Violence:
Teach Peace, Not War

September 13, 2001

Open the *Washington Post* to it's editorial pages, and war talk dominates.

Henry Kissinger: Destroy the Network.

Robert Kagan: We Must Fight This War.

Charles Krauthammer: To War, Not to Court.

William S. Cohen: American Holy War.

There is no column by Colman McCarthy talking peace.

From 1969 to 1997, McCarthy wrote a column for the *Washington Post*. He was let go because the column, he was told, wasn't making enough money for the company. "The market has spoken," was the way Robert Kaiser, the managing editor at the *Post*, put it at the time.

McCarthy is a pacifist. "I'm opposed to any kind of violence—economic, political, military, domestic."

But McCarthy is not surprised by the war talk coming from the Post. He has just completed an analysis of 430 opinion pieces that ran in the *Washington Post* in June, July and August 2001.

Of the 430 opinion pieces, 420 were written by right-wingers or centrists. Only ten were written by columnists one might consider left.

Nor is he surprised by the initial response of the American people to Tuesday's horrific attacks on innocent civilians. According to a Washington Post/ABC News poll, nine of ten people supported taking military action against the groups or nations responsible for the attacks "even if it led to war."

"In the flush of emotions, that is the common reaction," McCarthy says.

"But is it a rational and sane reaction?"

So, how should we respond?

"We forgive you. Please forgive us."

Forgive us for what?

"Please forgive us for being the most violent government on earth," McCarthy says. "Martin Luther King said this on April 4, 1967 at Riverside Church in New York. He said 'my government is the world's leading purveyor of violence.'"

What should Bush do?

"He should say that the United States will no longer be the world's largest seller of weapons, that we will begin to decrease our extravagantly wasteful military budget, which runs now at about $9,000 a second."

What will Bush do?

"Within the week, we will be bombing somebody somewhere," McCarthy says. "This is what his father did, this is what Clinton did."

"In the past 20 years, we have bombed Libya, Grenada, Panama, Somalia, Haiti, Afghanistan, Sudan, Iraq, and Yugoslavia. There are two things about those countries—all are poor countries, and the majority are people of dark colored skin."

Are you saying that we should just turn the other cheek?

"No, that's passivity," McCarthy says. "Pacifism is not passivity. Pacifism is direct action, direct resistance, refusing to cooperate with violence. That takes a lot of bravery. It takes much more courage than to use a gun or drop a bomb."

Since leaving the *Post*, McCarthy has dedicated his life to teaching peace. He has created the Center for Teaching Peace, which he runs out of his home in Northwest Washington. He teaches peace and non-violence at six area universities and at a number of public secondary and high schools.

But he's up against a system that systematically teaches violence—from that all pervasive teacher of children—television—to the President of the United States.

"In 1999, the day after the Columbine shootings, Bill Clinton went to a high school in Alexandria, Virginia and gave a speech to the school's Peer Mediation Club," McCarthy says.

"Clinton said 'we must teach our children to express their anger and resolve their conflicts with words not weapons.'"

"It was a great speech, but he went back that same night and ordered up the most intense bombing of Belgrade since that war began four weeks before."

Message to children: kid's violence is bad, but America's violence is good.

McCarthy says we should teach our children forgiveness, not to demonize people who have a grievance.

"When you hit your child, or beat up the person you are living with, you are saying— 'I want you to change the way you think or behave and I'm going to use physical force to make you change your way or your mind,'" he says.

"In fact, violence is rarely effective. If violence was effective, we would have had a peaceful planet eons ago."

How to break the cycle of violence?

"The same way you break the cycle of ignorance—educate people," McCarthy responds.

"Kids walk in the school with no idea that two plus two equals four. They are ignorant. We repeat over and over—Billy, two plus two equals four. And Billy leaves school knowing two plus two equals four. But he doesn't leave school knowing that an eye for an eye means we all go blind."

"We have about 50 million students in this country," McCarthy says. "Nearly all of those are going to graduate absolutely unaware of the philosophy of Gandhi, King, Dorothy Day, Howard Zinn, or A.J. Muste."

When he speaks before college audiences, McCarthy holds up a $100 dollar bill and says "I'll give this to anybody in the audience who can identify these next six people—Who was Robert E. Lee, Ulysses S. Grant, and Paul Revere? All hands go up on all three."

"Then I ask—Who was Jeanette Rankin (first women member of Congress, voted against World War I and World War II, said 'you can no more win a war than win an earthquake')

Dorothy Day (co-founder of the Catholic Worker movement), Ginetta Sagan (founder of Amnesty USA)?"

"The last three are women peacemakers. The first three are all male peacebreakers. The kids know the militarists. They don't know the peacemakers."

He hasn't lost his $100 bill yet to a student.

Of the 3,100 colleges and universities in the country, only about 70 have degree programs in peace studies and most are underfunded.

Instead of bombing, we should start teaching peace.

"We are graduating students as peace illiterates who have only heard of the side of violence," McCarthy laments. "If we don't teach our children peace, somebody else will teach them violence."

[The Center for Teaching Peace has produced two text books, Solutions to Violence and Strength Through Peace, both edited by Colman McCarthy. Each book contains 90 essays by the world's great theorists and practitioners of non-violence. ($25 each). To contact Colman McCarthy, write to: Center for Teaching Peace, 4501 Van Ness Street, N.W., Washington, D.C. 20016 Phone: (202) 537-1372]

Bowling for Baghdad

October 18, 2002

Last week, your nation's capital was a bit more surreal than usual.

First and foremost, there is the sniper.

And just when the sniper arrives in the neighborhood, here comes Michael Moore with his much awaited critique of violence in America—*Bowling for Columbine*.

We have three words of advice: go see it.

In one scene, Moore, a lifetime member of the National Rifle Association, goes to door to door in Toronto, Canada, doesn't knock, and just walks in.

Apparently, in Canada, many people don't lock their doors.

This in a country, Canada, where there are 7 million guns for a population of 33 million.

But in Canada there are fewer than 400 gun deaths a year.

In the United States, we hit 400 in two weeks—that's 11,000 gun deaths a year.

In the U.S., eight children under the age of 18 are killed by guns in America every day.

Moore raises a disturbing question: if it's just the guns, stupid, then how come Canadians are not slaughtering themselves the way we are slaughtering ourselves?

This question takes Moore to Littleton, Colorado, the site of the Columbine massacre, home to the war machine Lockheed Martin, the war machine that sponsors the news on National Public Radio.

There he interviews a spokesperson for Lockheed Martin, who tells Moore that the weapons the company builds there are used by the United States for defensive purposes.

Moore then cues up the war footage and runs through the history of U.S. aggression throughout the world—from Central American, to the Middle East, to Southeast Asia.

This juxtaposition of government and corporate violence with grainy film from the Columbine school's security camera capturing young children massacring young children drives home Moore's larger point—that the violence and duplicity in our society starts at the top.

Which brings us back to our nation's capital, where both parties' leadership, in part at the urging of the military-industrial-complex, gave the green light last week for a pre-emptive attack on Iraq.

We attended a press conference held by House Minority Leader Richard Gephardt (D-Missouri), the day after Gephardt went to the White House, stood by Bush, and gave the green light for war.

We had with us an editorial from that morning's *St. Louis Post Dispatch* titled "Gephardt Caves." Our sentiment exactly.

In it, Gephardt's hometown paper said that the reason he sided with Bush was because he wanted to be Speaker of the House, and then President. (This pattern, by the way, followed for other Democratic presidential hopefuls—Tom Daschle (D-South Dakota), Hillary Clinton (D-New York), John Kerry (D-Massachusetts), Joseph Lieberman (D-Connecticut), Diane Feinstein (D-California), John Edwards (D-North Carolina)—all of whom voted with Bush on the war.)

All said it was not about politics—not when young (American) lives are at stake.

But the *Post-Dispatch* called Gephardt on it.

Gephardt "protests too much when he says he is rising about politics."

"He wants to be speaker of the House—or president," the *Post-Dispatch* wrote. "He can't achieve either goal taking an unpopular stand against a war against Saddam."

We asked Gephardt whether he wanted be speaker or President.

"That's irrelevant," he shot back.

Not.

We then went over to the White House, where Ari Fleischer was conducting one of his press briefings.

We wanted to know about a two-sentence letter from Theodore Sorensen, the former legal advisor to President John F. Kennedy, that was published in the New York Times.

Sorensen wrote this:

"President Bush has not yet openly reprimanded his press secretary, Ari Fleischer, for suggesting that 'a bullet' is the cheapest way of accomplishing his goal of regime change in Iraq. Is it possible that the United States now endorses for other countries a policy of presidential assassination, the very epitome of terrorism, after our own tragic experience with that despicable act?"

So, Ari, did the President reprimand you?

Ari says: "As far as that is concerned, on the policy, as you know—I think you were here when I said on the record that that is not—and people heard it the day I said it—that is not a statement of administration policy."

But did the President reprimand you for saying that?

Ari says: "I think I have made the views clear of where the White House is on this."

Not.

We then head back over to the Congress, where the war-mongerer Senator Lieberman was releasing a Senate Governmental Affairs report on why Enron happened.

The conclusion: "All the public and private agencies that were supposed to exercise oversight and protect investors failed miserably."

The report was especially critical of the Securities and Exchange Commission (SEC) for failing to review any of Enron's annual reports after its 1997 filing. Before going over to the Lieberman briefing, we rang up former SEC chair Arthur Levitt.

We asked Levitt what we should ask Lieberman.

"Ask him—where was Lieberman?" Levitt told us. "He was

busy tying up the SEC in knots over auditors' independence, over the budget, and over options accounting."

We put this to Lieberman.

Lieberman gets testy and shoots back:

"Well, I hope he didn't say that, and if he did, it is grossly unfair and inaccurate."

Actually, quite fair and accurate.

Michael Moore is a political agitator.

Go to see his movie—and take as many friends and family members with you as possible.

Gephardt, Lieberman and Bush are political leaders.

Listen to them, and you can only get angry—and then organize to kick these guys out of office.

12 Reasons to Oppose a War with Iraq

February 20, 2003

Millions of people around the world last weekend demonstrated against a war on Iraq.

There was no mistaking the message: No war.

But, particularly with the airwaves and op-ed pages dominated by warmongers who mock and mischaracterize the burgeoning peace movement, there remains a need to continually reiterate the common-sense reasons to oppose a war. Here are a dozen:

1. Iraq is no threat to the United States.

With one of the weakest militaries in the region, Iraq is surely no threat to the world's lone superpower. There is no evidence it has or is close to having a nuclear capacity. There is no evidence that it has the means to launch a chemical and biological attack against the United States, if in fact it has such weaponry. There is no evidence of any Iraqi connection to al-Qaeda.

2. Iraq is deterrable.

Even if it had the means to threaten the United States, Iraq would be deterred by the certainty of an overwhelming military response in event of any attack on the United States. That Iraq is deterrable is shown by its decision not to use chemical or biological weapons (CBW) against the United States or Israel in the Gulf War.

3. Iraq's only conceivable threat to the United States is in event of war.

"Baghdad for now appears to be drawing a line short of conducting terrorist attacks with conventional or CBW against the United States," wrote CIA Director George Tenet in an October 2002 letter to Congress. "Should Saddam conclude that a U.S.-led attack could no longer be deterred, he probably would become much less constrained in adopting terrorist actions."

4. Other terrorist risks rise in event of war.

A U.S. attack and subsequent occupation of Iraq will provide new inspiration—and new recruitment fodder—for al-Qaeda or other terrorist groups, and will stimulate a long-term increased risk of terrorism, either on U.S. soil or against U.S. citizens overseas.

5. U.S. soldiers are vulnerable to chemical or biological attack in a war.

Although there is little reason to doubt the U.S. military will triumph relatively quickly in event of a war, U.S. soldiers face non-negligible risk of casualty. House-to-house fighting in Baghdad would be perilous.

If Bush administration accusations that Saddam maintains a CBW capacity are true, and if its claims of intelligence showing Iraqi plans to use CBW in event of war are both non-fabricated and accurate, then U.S. soldiers are at major risk. Last Sunday, 60 Minutes reported that army investigations show between 60 and 90 percent of its CBW protective gear malfunction. A Pentagon spokesperson actually suggested that holes in gas masks could easily be covered by duct tape.

6. Inspections can work.

To whatever extent Iraq maintains weapons of mass destruction, it is clear that the previous inspections process succeeded in destroying the overwhelming proportion. Iraqi intransigence notwithstanding, inspectors are now making progress. Despite the histrionics of the administration, past experience suggests the inspection process can work and finish the job.

7. Common sense says: Err on the side of non-violence.

Since Iraq poses no imminent threat to the United States nor any of its neighbors, it makes sense to continue to give inspections a chance. War can always be resorted to later. But once a war is commenced, the opportunity to achieve legitimate objectives without violence are lost. In addition to the obvious costs, the use of violence tends to beget more violence, spurring a highly unpredictable cycle.

8. The doctrine of preventative war is a threat to international law and humanity.

Conceding there is no imminent threat to the United States, the administration has sought to justify the war under a doctrine of preemptive, or preventative, action. But if it were legitimate to start a war because of what another country might do sometime in the future, then there would be very little legal or moral constraint on war-making. This proposition is dangerous and immoral.

9. Reject empire.

Many of the leading proponents of a war are motivated by desire to demonstrate U.S. military might, and commence an era when U.S. military power is exercised more routinely to satisfy the whims of elite U.S. factions. Many proponents now overtly defend the idea of U.S. imperialism, justified on the grounds that the United States—apparently unique among all previous aspirants to imperial authority—is motivated by promotion of democracy and human rights. But all empires have proffered such self-serving rationalizations to legitimize narrow self-interest. The present case is no different. Imperialism is fundamentally incompatible with democracy.

10. Revenge is not a legitimate motive for war.

There seems little doubt that part of the Bush administration motivation for war is the desire to "get" Saddam, since he refused to go away after the Gulf War and allegedly targeted the president's father. Saddam is an awful and brutal dictator, and an assassination attempt, if there was one, is a heinous act. But revenge should be no basis for war.

11. There are better solutions to our energy problems.

It overstates the case to say a war with Iraq would be a war for oil. There are too many other contributing factors to the rush to war. At the same time, it is not credible to claim designs on Iraqi oil are not part of calculus. And it is hard to see the United States caring much about Iraq if the country did not sit on the world's second largest oil reserves. But it is past time for the United States (and the rest of the world) to move beyond oil and carbon-based sources of energy. Existing efficiency technologies and renewable energy sources, if deployed, could dramatically reduce reliance on conventional energy sources; and modest investments in renewables could soon move us away from an oil-based economy.

12. Iraqi lives are at stake.

Unless a war brings immediate abdication by Saddam, military action is sure to cause massive casualties among Iraqi conscripts and especially among Iraqi civilians. Solidarity with the Iraqi people—not their brutal government, but the people—requires opposition to a war almost certain to cause them enormous suffering.

The Unbalanced Hawks at the *Washington Post*

March 4, 2003

What is going on at the *Washington Post?*

We would say that the *Post* editorial pages have become an outpost of the Defense Department—except that there is probably more dissent about the pending war in Iraq in the Pentagon than there is on the Post editorial pages.

In February alone, the *Post* editorialized nine times in favor of war, the last of those a full two columns of text, arguing against the considerable critical reader response the page had received for pounding the drums of war.

Over the six-month period from September through February, the leading newspaper in the nation's capital has editorialized 26 times in favor of war. It has sometimes been critical of the Bush administration, it has sometimes commented on developments in the drive to war without offering an opinion on the case for war itself, but it has never offered a peep against military action in Iraq.

The op-ed page, which might offer some balance, has also been heavily slanted in favor of war.

In February, the *Post* op-ed page ran 34 columns that took a position on the war: 24 favored war and 10 were opposed, at least in part. (Another 22 mentioned Iraq, and sometimes were focused exclusively on Iraq, but didn't clearly take a position for or against the war.)

Over the last four months, the *Post* has run 46 op-ed pieces favoring the war, and only 21 opposed.

This constitutes a significant change from September and October, when the opinion pieces were much more balanced, and even tilted slightly in favor of peace.

A few words on our methodology: We reviewed every editorial and op-ed piece in the *Post* over the last six months that contained the word "Iraq." We looked at the substance of the articles, and did not pre-judge based on the author. We categorized as neutral pieces which mentioned Iraq as an aside, or which discussed the war without taking a position. For example, an article which assesses how European countries are responding to U.S. Iraq-related proposals, but does not take a position on the war itself, is categorized as neutral. Neutral articles are not included in our tally.

The methodology tends to undercount pro-war columns. We categorized as neutral articles which we thought presumed a certain position on the war, but which did not explicitly articulate it. Over the last four months, there were 17 "neutral" articles which we believe had a pro-war slant, and only five "neutral" pieces with an anti-war orientation.

Our methodology also tended to overcount pro-peace op-eds. We tallied an op-ed as pro-peace if it took a position opposing the drive to war on the issue of the moment—even if the author made clear that they favored war on slightly different terms than the President proposed at the time (for example, if UN authorization was obtained).

Someone else reviewing the Post editorial page might disagree with our categorization of this or that article. We concede it may be rough around the edges. But overall, we think other reviewers would agree that our count is in the ballpark, and tends to underestimate the disparity between pro- and anti-war pieces.

Moreover, the dramatic quantitative tilt in favor of the war if anything underplays how pro-war the Post's editorial pages have been.

Among the regular columnists at the Post, those providing pieces that we considered anti-war include E.J. Dionne, a self-described "doubter" not opponent of the war, Mary McGrory, who pronounced herself convinced by Colin Powell's presentation to the United Nations (a position from which she has backtracked) and Richard Cohen, who actually is pro-war. Only

William Rasberry could be labeled a genuine and consistent opponent of war.

On the other side, the regular pro-war columnists are extraordinarily harsh and shrill. George Will labeled David Bonior and James McDermott, two congresspeople who visited Iraq, "American collaborators" with and "useful idiots" for Saddam. Michael Kelly, in one of his calmer moments, says no "serious" person can argue the case for peace. Charles Krauthammer says that those who call for UN authorization of U.S. military action in Iraq are guilty of a "kind of moral idiocy."

The *Post* op-ed page has been full of attacks on anti-war protesters. Richard Cohen has managed to author attacks on John Le Carre, for an anti-war column he wrote, poets against the war, and Representative Dennis Kucinich. Cohen joined war-monger Richard Perle in calling Kucinich a "liar" (or at very least a "fool"), because Kucinich suggested the war might be motivated in part by a U.S. interest in Iraqi oil. (Is this really a controversial claim? Pro-war *New York Times* columnist Thomas Friedman says that to deny a U.S. war in Iraq is partly about oil is "laughable.")

Neither Le Carre, the poets, nor Kucinich has been given space on the *Post* op-ed page.

Indeed, virtually no one who could be considered part of the peace movement has been given space. The only exceptions: A column by Hank Perritt, then a Democratic congressional candidate from Illinois, appeared in September. Morton Halperin argued the case for containment over war in February. And Reverend Bob Edgar, a former member of Congress who now heads the National Council of Churches, a key mover in the anti-war movement, was permitted a short piece that appeared in the week between Christmas and New Year's, when readership and attention to serious issues is at a lowpoint.

Edgar only was given the slot after editorial page editor Fred Hiatt, in an op-ed, characterized the anti-war movement, and Edgar by name, as "Saddam's lawyers."

Does this shockingly one-sided treatment on the *Post* editorial pages of the major issue of the day matter?

It matters a lot.

The *Washington Post* and the *New York Times* are the two papers that most fundamentally set the boundaries for legitimate opinion in Washington, D.C. The extraordinary tilt for war in the *Post* editorial pages in the last four months makes it harder for officialdom in Washington and the Establishment generally to speak out against war.

Everyone who might be characterized as an "insider" in the political-military-corporate establishment knows there are major internal divisions on the prospect of war among elder statesmen, retired military brass and present-day corporate CEOs. There are many reasons those voices are inhibited from speaking out, but the *Post's* extremist editorial pages are certainly a real contributor.

The failure to give a prominent platform to anti-war voices has also worked to soften the debate among the citizenry. It's no answer to say a vibrant anti-war movement, reliant on the Internet, its own communications channels and dissenting voices in other major media outlets, has sprung up. Sending out an e-mail missive is not exactly the same thing as publishing an op-ed in the Washington Post.

The *Post* editorial page editors have failed to fulfill their duty to democracy. The heavy slant on the editorial pages, the extreme pro-war rhetoric offset only by hedging and uncertain war critics, and the scurrilous attacks on the anti-war movement to which minimal response has been permitted—all have undermined rather than fueled a robust national debate.

At this point, there is no real way for the Post to rectify its wrongdoing. It could start to mitigate the effect by immediately making a conscious effort to solicit and publish a disproportionately high number of pro-peace op-eds, and to let the peace movement occasionally speak for itself, especially since the paper's regular columnists so savagely and repeatedly attack it.

Unfortunately, the drive to war, which the Post editorial pages have helped fuel, may not stop in Iraq. There is good reason to believe that a war with Iraq will be followed by calls from the hawks at the *Post* and around the administration for more military action, against some other target. Will the paper's editorial page editors find a better way to achieve balance in advance of the next military buildup? Or are the paper's editorial pages now simply devoted to the Permanent War Campaign?

Other Things You Might Do With $87 Billion

September 10, 2003

You can actually get a few things done with $87 billion, the amount that President Bush has asked Congress to appropriate for expenditures related to the military occupation and reconstruction of Iraq.

For example:

The World Health Organization (WHO) and other UN bodies estimate the cost of providing treatment and prevention services in developing countries for tuberculosis, HIV/AIDS and malaria at $12 billion a year.

The WHO Commission on Macroeconomics and Health estimated that donor investment of $27 billion a year, including expenditures on TB, AIDS and malaria, as well as to eliminate death and suffering from other infectious diseases and nutritional deficiencies, could save 8 million lives a year. That's eight million lives. A year.

The UN Development Program estimated in 1998 that the annual additional cost of achieving basic education for all was $6 billion.

Prefer to spend some or all of the money at home? Even in the United States, where the dollar doesn't go as far, $87 billion can perform some pretty impressive feats.

For example, according to Business Leaders for Sensible Priorities, it would only cost $6 billion a year to provide health insurance to all uninsured children in the United States. You can provide Head Start and Early Head Start to all eligible children for $8 billion annually. You can reduce class size to 15 students per teacher in all first-, second- and third-grade classrooms for $11 billion a year.

For $87 billion, you could eliminate the backlog of maintenance needs at national parks nearly 15 times over. You could cover more than half the Environmental Protection Agency

(EPA)-estimated 20-year investment needs to ensure safe drinking water throughout the United States. You could more than double the annual capital expenditures needed to improve public transportation in the United States, according to estimates of the American Association of State Highway and Transportation Officials. You could provide almost half of the overall funding EPA says is needed to provide clean watersheds in the United States, including through wastewater treatment, sewer upgrades and nonpoint source pollution control.

It just so happens, as the Center for Budget and Policy Priorities points out, that $87 billion is almost exactly what all departments in the federal government combined spend annually on education, training, employment and social services. So you could fund that for a year.

If you looked at the $87 billion as found money, and wanted to do something unorthodox, you could eliminate California's state budget deficit two times over.

And, you would still have enough left over to enable the Detroit Tigers (baseball's worst team) next year to field a team full of Alex Rodriguez's. (Rodriguez, at $25 million a year, is baseball's highest-paid player. A full roster—25 players—of Rodriguez's would cost $625 million.)

We accept that having imposed devastating economic sanctions on Iraq for a decade and twice waged war on the country, the United States has a major obligation to support reconstruction in Iraq. But three-quarters of the president's request is for military expenses, not reconstruction, the request follows a previous $79 billion appropriation, additional requests are certain to follow, and much of the money being spent on reconstruction is being funneled as poorly scrutinized corporate welfare to Bush and Vice President Cheney's buddies at companies like Halliburton and Bechtel.

If one steps back for a moment, it is evident that there is a long list of expenditures that would do more to improve the world, and more to improve U.S. security if reasonably defined, than what the president proposes to do in Iraq.

A strange circumstance has evolved in the United States. Military expenditures can be justified at almost any level. ("Whatever it takes to defend freedom.") Politicians don't say, "Whatever it takes to make sure every child in this country has a decent education." Or, "Whatever it takes to deal with the worst health pandemic in the history of the world (HIV/AIDS)." When it comes to the military, there is neither a sense of proportion, nor of trade offs.

This state of affairs is a tribute to the military contractors and political leaders who have ridden to power by instilling fear in the populace. It can be traced in no small part to campaign contributions and lobbyist influence, but the problem runs much deeper than that. Fear has penetrated deep into the culture.

But the administration's overreach in Iraq now offers an opportunity to create a new sense of priorities. It is now even more apparent than it was before the war that Iraq posed no security threat to the United States. And the sums of money requested by the administration—and more will be coming—are so extraordinary that they practically demand consideration of alternative expenditures.

After all, you really can do quite a bit with $87 billion.

PART EIGHT

THE WORST

Multinational Monitor winds down every year by publishing the 10 Worst Corporations of the Year.

It's a challenge to pick and choose among the polluters, union-busters and food poisoners, to highlight the worst of the clear-cutters, price-gougers and fraudsters, to select only some of the companies who have employed brutalized child labor, fired whistleblowers, violated privacy, or killed its workers or consumers.

In this area, making determinations between bad and worse is never easy. We don't claim to follow a scientific process. We try to highlight a diverse array of corporate wrongdoing, not to pick the same companies every year, and rely on our best judgement.

We go through the process not just to focus attention on the worst of the worst, but also to highlight how the most egregious corporate abuses are representative of generalized corporate practices.

Yes, a 2002 federal indictment against the accounting firm Arthur Andersen alledged that "tons of paper relating to the Enron audit were promptly shredded as part of the orchestrated document destruction," with Andersen shredders unable to handle the workload. But how different were the company's actions from the recommendations offered by former Securities and Exchange Commission Chair Harvey Pitt, who a few years before taking office had advised, "Each comapny should have a system of determining the retention and destruction of documents?"

Sure, Safeway demanded outrageous givebacks from its workers in contract negotiations in 2003. But so did the rest of the Southern California grocery chains, who imposed sympathy lockouts of their unionized workers. And these companies still provide better jobs than those offered by retailing colossus Wal-Mart, which is threatening to enter the market.

The Ten Worst Corporations of 1999

December 30, 1999

Charles Dickens, where are you when we need you?

Never has "It was the best of times, it was the worst of times" served as a more apt commentary on society than today.

The NASDAQ just broke 4,000 and has nearly doubled in 1999. The Dow is at near-record heights as well. Internet, computer and communications technologies are evolving at a stunning velocity. A lot of people are becoming incredibly wealthy, and a lot are having fun on the Internet.

If you want, you can look at this state of affairs and say that everything is fine. Go ahead, pat yourself on the back.

Or, you can look at a different set of snapshots and ask these and many other probing questions:

Why does the United States, the richest nation in the history of the world, warehouse its elderly in what are euphemistically called nursing homes, permitting many to live out their last years in social isolation and sometimes filth and neglect?

Why are profitable and fast-growing corporations permitted to expose their workers to dangerous and life-threatening conditions that could be avoided with minimal investments?

Why are the poor, undereducated and unsophisticated subject to a host of financial scams that empty their small savings accounts or throw them into debt?

Why are working people in the United State who try to organize into unions regularly subjected to threats of firing and plant closure, harassment, intimidation and managerial refusal to bargain with duly elected unions?

Why does the United States permit the massive concentration of economic and political power through mergers and acquisitions that work to foreclose democratic options for the future?

Why do rich societies permit their corporations to engage,

directly or indirectly, through contractors and subcontractors, in brutally exploitative practices in developing countries—practices that have long been outlawed in the rich countries?

Why indeed.

There is of course no one single answer to these and the many other critical questions that should be asked in a society that does so much to generate wealth, at least as measured by conventional standards, but so little to distribute that wealth—or justice—evenly. But there is one connecting theme that serves, at least, as a partial answer to many of these questions: concentrated corporate power.

Each year, to highlight the consequences of corporations and greed run amok, *Multinational Monitor* publishes a list of the 10 worst corporations of the year.

Here's this year's list, in alphabetical order:

Avondale: Good riddance

For more than half a decade, Avondale, which operates a shipyard in New Orleans, waged a vicious campaign to block recognition of its employees' desire for a union—a desire springing in no small part from way below industry standard wages and a gruesome workplace casualty record of a death a year. In August, Avondale was acquired by Litton, which agreed to recognize the workers' union in November.

Citigroup: The standard in political corruption

Citigroup played the lead role in ushering the "Financial Services Modernization Act" through the U.S. Congress, in the process joining with the rest of the financial services industry to set a new standard in legalized bribery. The Act will tear down the regulatory walls between banks, and insurance companies and securities firms, paving the massive concentration of financial wealth and a future of industry bailouts, weakening the Community Reinvestment Act and permitting huge intrusions on consumer privacy.

Del Monte: Banana imperialism into the twenty-first century

In September, Bandegua, the Guatemalan subsidiary of Coral Gables, Florida-based Fresh Del Monte Produce (now a separate company from California-based Del Monte Foods), dismissed 900 of its banana workers. When other unionized Bandegua workers tried to organize a solidarity protest, the union leadership was met with a 200-person, armed goon squad which chased the leadership out of town, threatening to kill them if they returned. Del Monte and Bandegua deny responsibility, but they have certainly benefited from the threats.

Guardian Postacute: Maggots everywhere.

After learning that of Guardian Postacute Services Inc., a San Francisco Bay area nursing home chain, had permitted dirty feeding tubes to be installed into patients who then became infested with maggots, had permitted patients to lie for extended periods in their urine and feces, and had failed to take strong action against an employee who sexually abused patients, Santa Clara County Deputy District Attorney Randy Hey has filed criminal charges against Guardian.

Hoffman La Roche: Take the market, pay the fine

Earlier this year, the Swiss pharmaceutical giant F. Hoffmann-La Roche Ltd. paid $500 million—the largest fine in U.S. antitrust history—for its efforts with German chemical maker BASF to allocate market shares for certain vitamins sold in the United States and elsewhere. The whistleblower who inspired the case says Roche's response to the fines was to redouble its efforts to gain total control of the vitamin market.

Tosco: Four dead workers

On February 23, 1999, four workers at a Tosco Corp. facility in Avon, California were burned to death after they tried to replace a leaky oil pipe. The San Francisco Chronicle reported that one Tosco employee, Anthony Creggett, claimed shortly after the fire that plant managers had refused a request by four workers to shut down the high-temperature distillation tower during the repairs on the pipe.

Tyson: Seven deaths in seven months

Maybe we should consider raising our own chickens. Clearly, relying on multinational corporations to raise millions of birds for us in unsanitary and dangerous conditions is not working out. Tysons Foods is a case in point. Do you really want to buy your chicken from these people? Consider this: seven workers have been killed at Tyson facilities this year. There have been no reported job-related deaths at any other poultry company in 1999.

U.S. Bank: Big brother is watching

Earlier this year, U.S. Bank agreed to stop selling its customers' personal data—everything from social security numbers to account balances, from birth date to number of credit cards—to a telemarketing firm. But that came only after Minnesota Attorney General Mike Hatch filed a lawsuit against U.S. Bank, alleging it violated the federal Fair Credit Reporting Act and engaged in consumer fraud and deceptive advertising.

Whirlpool: Preying on the poor

Earlier this year, an Alabama jury hit a recently spun off Whirlpool subsidiary, Whirlpool Financial, and one of its dealers with a $581 million verdict for targeting illiterate and poor people in a sales scheme involving satellite television dishes. Lawyers representing the victims said that Whirlpool had dealers all over the state going door-to-door soliciting poor, unsophisticated and elderly customers to purchase satellite television dishes for $1,100 plus 22 percent interest. The same equipment could be bought at an electronics store for $199. On appeal, an Alabama appellate court agreed only to knock the verdict down to $301 million.

W.R. Grace: You can't eat enough of it

At least 192 people have died of asbestos-related disease from a mine near Libby, Montana that was owned by W.R. Grace for nearly 30 years, according to a report that appeared in the Seattle Post-Intelligencer. At least another 375 have been diagnosed with the fatal disease. For three decades, Grace mined enormous deposits of vermiculite in the earth of nearby

Zonolite Mountain. Under the vermiculite are millions of tons of tremolite, a rare and exceedingly toxic form of asbestos. Community residents say Grace for years told residents and workers that the dust was harmless. "When my father was a young man they told him, 'You can't eat enough of that stuff. It won't bother you. He's dead,'" Patrick Vinion, a Libby resident, says. Now Vinion, who never worked as a miner, is himself dying from asbestos-related disease.

New Century, Same as the Old Century: The Ten Worst Corporations of 2000

December 27, 2000

Self-regulation is all the rage in Washington, D.C. these days.

Responsible corporations, perhaps working in conjunction with government, can band together to devise standards of ethical conduct that will protect people and the planet, without unnecessary costs—that's the line among a wide array of beltway players. And with Christine Todd Whitman anointed to head up the Environmental Protection Agency, it's going to become even more faddish.

There's one problem with the self-regulation theory: it doesn't work.

Every corporation regulates itself. It chooses whether to obey the law, or not. It chooses whether to permit its employees to unionize, or to fight organizing efforts, whether to bargain fairly with unions, or to try to bust them. It chooses whether to use clean production technologies, or to pollute.

The self-regulation record is clear. Too often, corporations choose to despoil the natural environment, deny care to the sick, smash workers' unions, retaliate against whistleblowers who seek to call attention egregious corporate abuses, endanger consumers, and more.

Need evidence? That's why *Multinational Monitor* publishes its annual list of the Ten Worst Corporations of the Year. Appearing on this year's list:

Aventis: Making Human Guinea Pigs

The biotech company recklessly raced its genetically modified StarLink corn to market. Not approved for human consumption, Starlink soon found its way into the food supply (through Taco Bell shells and other food items), through cross-pollination with conventional corn crops, improper mixing in grain elevators or otherwise. Critics say StarLink corn poses serious allergenic risks, including fever, rashes and diarrhea.

BAT: Smuggler of Death

Industry documents uncovered in connection with the U.S. state litigation against the tobacco industry reveal that British American Tobacco for decades promoted and facilitated a worldwide cigarette smuggling scheme, with extensive efforts in Latin America and Asia. Cigarette smuggling evades excise taxes—lowering cigarette prices and increasing smoking rates.

BP/Amoco: Lawbreaker

The oil giant which likes to portray itself as environmentally responsible paid major fines and entered settlements in 2000 for illegal disposal of hazardous waste, alleged Clean Air Act violations, and underpaying royalties for oil produced on federal and Native American lands.

DoubleClick: Cookie Crook?

DoubleClick is rubbing up against the edge of Internet privacy protections, having acquired the ability to match consumer information from web usage and purchases—mostly gained without consumer knowledge or informed consent—with consumers' names and addresses.

Ford/Firestone: Reckless Homicide?

Ford and Firestone placed the lethal combination of Ford Explorers and Firestone tires on the road, leaving the deadly mix on the road even after they had overwhelming evidence of the consumer hazard.

Glaxo Wellcome: Patents Over People

With the HIV/AIDS crisis at least as severe as the Black Death which wracked Europe in medieval times, Glaxo Wellcome and other drug manufacturers persist in engaging in a variety of tactics to block African and other poor countries from making available cheap generic versions of lifesaving AIDS drugs.

Lockheed Martin: Testing Its Pollutant on Humans

The *Los Angeles Times* reported in November that on behalf of military contractor Lockheed Martin, Loma Linda University is conducting the first large-scale tests of a toxic drinking water contaminant—a rocket fuel component—on human subjects.

Phillips Petroleum: Deadly Employer

A massive explosion at a Phillips Petroleum plastics plant in Pasadena, Texas in March killed one person and injured 74. It was the third fatal accident at the sprawling petrochemical complex in the last 11 years, including a 1989 blast that killed 23 people and an explosion in June1999 that left two dead.

Smithfield Foods: Pig Out

To the detriment of family farmers, Smithfield Foods is rushing to consolidate control of the meatpacking industry, most recently with a proposed merger with IBP Inc. While wreaking havoc on the farm economy, the big hog companies are also destroying farm country. The rapid growth of factory farms and the resulting mountains of untreated livestock manure are fouling drinking water supplies and causing a public health risk throughout the United States.

Titan International: Union Buster

Approximately 1,000 United Steelworker of America (USWA) workers at two Titan facilities have struck the maker of agricultural, off-road and construction tires, wheels and assemblies since 1998. The viciously anti-union Titan CEO Morry Taylor responded to a National Labor Relations Board unfair labor practices complaint by reportedly telling the Natchez Democrat that "I figure in five years they'll get that to the first federal court. By that time they'll all be enjoying retirement pay."

And that's about as good a refutation of the idea of self-regulation as any.

(The full story, "The Ten Worst Corporation of the Year," is posted at http://www.essential.org/monitor/mm2000/00-december/enemies.html.)

The Ten Worst Corporations of 2001

January 2, 2002

In a year marked not only by the now-standard forms of corporate marauding but also by brazen wartime profiteering, it was no easy chore to identify *Multinational Monitor*'s 10 corporations of 2001.

The competition was even tougher than usual. But choices had to be made. And now decisions have been reached.

Multinational Monitor has named Abbott Laboratories, Argenbright, Bayer, Coke, Enron, Exxon Mobil, Philip Morris, Sara Lee, Southern Co. and Wal-Mart as the 10 worst corporations of 2001

Appearing in alphabetical order, the 10 worst are:

Abbott Laboratories, for its TAP Pharmaceuticals, a joint venture with Japanese Takeda Pharmaceuticals. TAP was forced to pay $875 million to resolve criminal charges and civil liability in connection with allegations of major Medicare reimbursement fraud. Among other alleged fraudulent activities, as a way of hooking doctors on prescribing Lupron, its prostate cancer drug, TAP gave doctors free samples and then encouraged doctors to bill Medicare for the free samples.

Argenbright, the security company, for repeat violations of regulations for airport security. Argenbright's appalling record—including violations of security rules it had been caught breaking just a year earlier—helped convince Congress to federalize U.S. airport security operations.

Bayer, for its overcharge of the government and public for the anti-anthrax drug Cipro, based on a patent monopoly that may well be improperly maintained by virtue of a collusive arrangement with a generic manufacturer. Bayer also secured a place on the 10 worst list for its dangerous peddling of antibiotics for poultry (contributing to antibiotic resistance among humans) and its harassment of a German watchdog group,

Coalition Against Bayer Dangers, for maintaining a BayerWatch.com website.

Coca Cola, for its sponsorship of the first Harry Potter movie and possible sequels, using a children's favorite to hawk its unhealthy product, and for alleged complicity with death squads in Colombia targeting union leaders there.

Enron, for costing many of its employees their life savings by refusing to let them dump company stock from their pension plans, as Enron plunged toward bankruptcy.

ExxonMobil, for leading the global warming denial campaign (even O'Dwyer's, a leading rag of the public relations industry, has chastised the company for its "stubborn refusal to acknowledge the fact that burning fossil fuels has a role in global warming") and blocking efforts at appropriate remedial action, plus a host of other reckless activities.

Philip Morris, for its "we've changed" marketing campaign—revealed to be a hoax by a Czech study it commissioned alleging cost savings from smoking-related premature deaths, as well as the company's ongoing efforts to addict millions of new smokers.

Sara Lee, for a scandal involving its Ball Park Franks hot dogs. Listeria-contaminated Ball Park Franks killed 21 and seriously injured 100 in 1998. In 2001, with civil and criminal litigation around the case heating up, the Detroit Free Press reported that Sara Lee stopped performing tests for bacteria after it started recording too many positives. The U.S. attorney, which handled prosecution of the criminal case, insists Sara Lee did not know about the presence of listeria in its hot dogs. In an extraordinary move, the U.S. attorney issued a joint press release with Sara Lee announcing settlement of the case. The final tally: 21 dead. A misdemeanor plea. A $200,000 fine.

Southern Co., the largest electric utility in the United States, for its efforts to defeat sensible air pollution regulations. Southern is a heavy user of coal, and leads the fight to maintain a ridiculous "grandfather" clause in the U.S. Clean Air Act, which exempts power plants built before 1970 from Clean Air Act standards.

Wal-Mart, for continuing to source products from overseas sweatshops, for viciously battling efforts to unionize any fraction of its workforce (the largest in the United States, among private employers), and for contributing to the sprawl that blights the U.S. landscape.

For a complete version of *Multinational Monitor's* article naming the 10 worst corporations of 2001, see www.essential.org/monitor.

The 10 Worst Corporations of 2002

January 2, 2003

2002 will forever be remembered as the year of corporate crime, the year even President George Bush embraced the notion of "corporate responsibility."

While the Bush White House has now downgraded its "corporate responsibility portal" to a mere link to uninspiring content on the White House webpage, and although the prospect of war has largely bumped the issue off the front pages, the cascade of corporate financial and accounting scandals continues.

We easily could have filled *Multinational Monitor's* list of the 10 Worst Corporations of the Year with some of the dozens of companies embroiled in the financial scandals.

But we decided against that course.

As extraordinary as the financial misconduct has been, we didn't want to contribute to the perception that corporate wrongdoing in 2002 was limited to the financial misdeeds arena.

For *Multinational Monitor's* 10 Worst Corporations of 2002 list, we included only Andersen from the ranks of the financial criminals and miscreants. Andersen's assembly line document destruction certainly merits a place on the list. (Citigroup appears on the list as well, but primarily for a subsidiary's involvement in predatory lending, as well as the company's funding of environmentally destructive projects around the world.)

As for the rest, we present a collection of polluters, dangerous pill peddlers, modern-day mercenaries, enablers of human rights abuses, merchants of death, and beneficiaries of rural destruction and misery.

Multinational Monitor has named Arthur Andersen, British American Tobacco (BAT), Caterpillar, Citigroup, DynCorp, M&M/Mars, Procter & Gamble, Schering Plough, Shell and

Wyeth as the 10 Worst Corporations of 2001.

Appearing in alphabetical order, the 10 worst are:

Arthur Andersen, for a massive scheme to destroy documents related to the Enron meltdown. "Tons of paper relating to the Enron audit were promptly shredded as part of the orchestrated document destruction," a federal indictment against Andersen alleged. "The shredder at the Andersen office at the Enron building was used virtually constantly and, to handle the overload, dozens of large trunks filled with Enron documents were sent to Andersen's main Houston office to be shredded." Andersen was convicted for illegal document destruction, effectively putting the company out of business.

BAT, for operating worldwide programs supposedly designed to prevent youth smoking but which actually make the practice more attractive to kids (by suggesting smoking is an adult activity), continuing to deny the harmful health effects of second-hand smoke, and working to oppose efforts at the World Health Organization to adopt a strong Framework Convention on Tobacco Control.

Caterpillar, for selling bulldozers to the Israeli Defense Forces (IDF), which are used as an instrument of war to destroy Palestinian homes and buildings. The IDF has destroyed more than 7,000 Palestinian homes since the beginning of the Israeli occupation in 1967, leaving 30,000 people homeless.

Citigroup, both for its deep involvement in the Enron and other financial scandals and its predatory lending practices through its recently acquired subsidiary The Associates. Citigroup paid $215 million to resolve Federal Trade Commission (FTC) charges that The Associates engaged in systematic and widespread deceptive and abusive lending practices.

DynCorp, a controversial private firm which subcontracts military services with the Defense Department, for flying planes that spray herbicides on coca crops in Colombia. Farmers on the ground allege that the herbicides are killing their legal crops, and exposing them to dangerous toxins.

M&M/Mars, for responding tepidly to revelations about child slaves in the West African fields where much of the world's cocoa is grown, and refusing to commit to purchase a modest 5 percent of its product from Fair Trade providers.

Procter & Gamble, the maker of Folger's coffee and part of the coffee roaster oligopoly, for failing to take action to address plummeting coffee bean prices. Low prices have pushed tens of thousands of farmers in Central America, Ethiopia, Uganda and elsewhere to the edge of survival, or destroyed their means of livelihood altogether.

Schering Plough, for a series of scandals, most prominently allegation of repeated failure over recent years to fix problems in manufacturing dozens of drugs at four of its facilities in New Jersey and Puerto Rico. Schering paid $500 million to settle the case with the Food and Drug Administration.

Shell Oil, for continuing business as usual as one of the world's leading environmental violators—while marketing itself as a socially and environmentally responsible company.

Wyeth, for using duplicitous means, and without sufficient scientific proof, to market hormone replacement therapy (HRT) to women as a fountain of youth. Scientific evidence reported in 2002 showed that long-term HRT actually threatens women's lives, by increasing the risks of breast cancer, heart attack, stroke and pulmonary embolism.

What's the lesson to draw from this year's 10 worst list? Not only are Enron, WorldCom, Adelphia, Tyco and the rest indicative of a fundamentally corrupt financial system, they are representative of a rotten system of corporate dominance.

The full 10 Worst Corporations of 2002 list is available at <http://www.multinationalmonitor.org>.

The 10 Worst Corporations of 2003

February 4, 2004

2003 was not a year of garden variety corporate wrongdoing. No, the sheer variety, reach and intricacy of corporate schemes, scandal and crimes was spellbinding. Not an easy year to pick the 10 worst companies, for sure.

But *Multinational Monitor* magazine cannot be deterred by such complications. And so, here follows, in alphabetical order, our list for *Multinational Monitor* of the 10 worst corporations of 2003.

Bayer: 2003 may be remembered as the year of the headache at Bayer. In May, the company agreed to plead guilty to a criminal count and pay more than $250 million to resolve allegations that it denied Medicaid discounts to which it was entitled. The company was beleaguered with litigation related to its anti-cholesterol drug Baycol. Bayer pulled the drug—which has been linked to a sometimes fatal muscle disorder—from the market, but is facing thousands of suits from patients who allege they were harmed by the drug. In June, the *New York Times* reported on internal company memos which appear to show that the company continued to promote the drug even as its own analysis had revealed the dangers of the product. Bayer denies the allegations.

Boeing: In one of the grandest schemes of corporate welfare in recent memory, Boeing engineered a deal whereby the Pentagon would lease tanker planes—767s that refuel fighter planes in the air—from Boeing. The pricetag of $27.6 billion was billions more than the cost of simply buying the planes. The deal may unravel, though, because the company in November fired for wrongdoing both the employee that negotiated the contract for Boeing (the company's chief financial officer), and the employee that negotiated the contract for the government. How could Boeing fire a Pentagon employee? Simple. She was no longer a Pentagon employee. Boeing had hired her shortly

after the company clinched the deal.

Brighthouse: A new-agey advertising/consulting/ strategic advice company, Brighthouse's claim to infamy is its Neurostrategies Institute, which undertakes research to see how the brain responds to advertising campaigns. In a cutting-edge effort to extend and sharpen the commercial reach in ways never previously before possible, the institute is using MRIs to monitor activity in people's brains triggered by advertisements.

Clear Channel: The radio behemoth Clear Channel specializes in consuming or squashing locally owned radio stations, imposing a homogenized music play list on once interesting stations, and offering cultural support for U.S. imperial adventures. It has also compiled a record of "repeated law-breaking," according to our colleague Jim Donahue, violating the law—including prohibitions on deceptive advertising and on broadcasting conversations without obtaining permission of the second party to the conversation—on 36 separate occasions over the previous three years.

Diebold: A North Canton, Ohio-based company that is one of the largest U.S. voting machine manufacturers, and an aggressive peddler of its electronic voting machines, Diebold has managed to demonstrate that it fails any reasonable test of qualifications for involvement with the voting process. Its CEO has worked as a major fundraiser for President George Bush. Computer experts revealed serious flaws in its voting technology, and activists showed how careless it was with confidential information. And it threatened lawsuits against activists who published on the Internet documents from the company showing its failures.

Halliburton: Now the owner of the company which initially drafted plans for privatization of U.S. military functions—plans drafted during the Bush I administration when current Vice President and former Halliburton CEO Dick Cheney was Secretary of Defense—Halliburton is pulling in billions in revenues for contract work—providing logistical support ranging from oil to food—in Iraq. Tens of millions, at least, appear to be overcharges. Some analysts say the charges for oil provision amount to "highway robbery."

HealthSouth: Fifteen of its top executives have pled guilty in connection with a multi-billion dollar scheme to defraud investors, the public and the U.S. government about the company's financial condition. The founder and CEO of the company that runs a network of outpatient surgery, diagnostic imagery and rehabilitative healthcare centers, Richard Scrushy, is fighting the charges. But thanks to the slick maneuvering of attorney Bob Bennett, it appears the company itself will get off scot free—no indictments, no pleas, no fines, no probation.

Inamed: The California-based company sought Food and Drug Administration approval for silicone breast implants, even though it was not able to present long-term safety data—the very thing that led the FDA to restrict sales of silicone implants a decade ago. In light of what remains unknown and what is known about the implants' effects—including painful breast hardening which can lead to deformity, and very high rupture rates—the FDA in January 2004 denied Inamed's application for marketing approval.

Merrill Lynch: This company keeps messing up. Fresh off of a $100 million fine levied because analysts were recommending stocks that they trashed in private e-mails, the company saw three former execs indicted for shady dealings with Enron. The company itself managed to escape with something less than a slap on the wrist—no prosecution in exchange for "oversight."

Safeway: One of the largest U.S. grocery chains, Safeway is leading the charge to demand givebacks from striking and locked out grocery workers in Southern California. Along with Albertsons and Ralphs (Kroger's), Safeway's Vons and Pavilion stores are asking employees to start paying for a major chunk of their health insurance. Under the company's proposals, workers and their families will lose $4,000 to $6,000 a year in health insurance benefits.

The Criminal Element

September 6, 1999

The criminal element has seeped deep into every nook and cranny of American society.

Forget about the underworld—these crooks dominate every aspect of our market, culture, and politics.

They cast a deep dark shadow over life in turn of the century America.

We buy gas from them (Exxon, Chevron, Unocal).

We take pictures with their cameras and film (Eastman Kodak).

We drink their beer (Coors).

We buy insurance from them to guard against financial catastrophe if we get sick (Blue Cross Blue Shield).

And then when we get sick, we buy pharmaceuticals from them (Pfizer, Warner Lambert, Ortho Pharmaceuticals).

We do our laundry in washers and dryers from them (General Electric).

We vacation with them (Royal Caribbean Cruise Lines).

We buy our food from them (Archer Daniels Midland, Southland, Tyson Foods, U.S. Sugar).

We drive with them (Hyundai) and fly with them (Korean Air Lines).

All of these companies and more turned up on *Corporate Crime Reporter's* list of the Top 100 Corporate Criminals of the 1990s, released this past week at a news conference at the National Press Club.

Standing before a roomful of reporters and cameras (including a C-Span camera which took us live to our TV nation), we made the following points:

Every year, the major business magazines put out their annual surveys of big business in America.

You have the Fortune 500, the Forbes 400, the Forbes Platinum 100, the International 800—among others.

These lists rank big corporations by sales, assets, profits and market share.

The point of these surveys is simple—to identify and glorify the biggest and most profitable corporations.

The point of releasing The Top 100 Corporate Criminals of the Decade, on the other hand, was to focus public attention on the pervasive criminality that has corrupted the marketplace and that is given little sustained attention and analysis by politicians and news outlets.

To compile The Top 100 Corporate Criminals of the 1990s, we used the most narrow and conservative of definitions—corporations that have pled guilty or no contest to crimes and have been criminally fined. And still, with the most narrow and conservative of definitions of corporate crime, we came up with society's most powerful actors.

Six corporations that made the list of the Top 100 Corporate Criminals were criminal recidivist companies during the 1990s.

Exxon, Royal Caribbean, Rockwell International, Warner-Lambert, Teledyne, and United Technologies each pled guilty to more than one crime during the 1990s.

And we warned that we in no way imply that these corporations are in any way the worst or have committed the most egregious crimes.

We did not try to assess and compare the damage committed by these corporate criminals or by other corporate wrongdoers.

We warned that companies that are criminally prosecuted represent only the tip of a very large iceberg of corporate wrongdoing.

For every company convicted of health care fraud, there are hundreds of others who get away with ripping off Medicare and Medicaid, or face only mild slap-on-the-wrist fines and civil penalties when caught.

For every company convicted of polluting the nation's

waterways, there are many others who are not prosecuted because their corporate defense lawyers are able to offer up a low-level employee to go to jail in exchange for a promise from prosecutors not to touch the company or high-level executives.

For every corporation convicted of bribery or of giving money directly to a public official in violation of federal law, there are thousands who give money legally through political action committees to candidates and political parties. They profit from a system that effectively has legalized bribery.

For every corporation convicted of selling illegal pesticides, there are hundreds more who are not prosecuted because their lobbyists have worked their way in Washington to ensure that dangerous pesticides remain legal.

For every corporation convicted of reckless homicide in the death of a worker, there are hundreds of others that don't even get investigated for reckless homicide when a worker is killed on the job. Only a few district attorneys across the country (Michael McCann, the DA in Milwaukee County, Wisconsin, being one) regularly investigate workplace deaths as homicides.

We pointed out that corporations define the laws under which they live.

An argument can be made that the most egregious wrongful corporate acts—the genetic engineering of the food supply, or the systematic pollution of the nation's air and waterways, or the bribery by corporate criminals of the political parties—are totally legal.

For your convenience, we print here the list of 100 crooks that fall well within a very conservative definition of criminality.

Carry this list wherever you go, and when the subject turns to crime, feel free to pull out the list and lash the criminal element.

THE TOP 100 CORPORATE CRIMINALS OF THE 1990S

1) F. Hoffmann-La Roche Ltd.
Type of Crime: Antitrust
Criminal Fine: $500 million

2) Daiwa Bank Ltd.
Type of Crime: Financial
Criminal Fine: $340 million

3) BASF Aktiengesellschaft
Type of Crime: Antitrust
Criminal Fine: $225 million

4) SGL Carbon Aktiengesellschaft (SGL AG)
Type of Crime: Antitrust
Criminal Fine: $135 million

5) Exxon Corporation and Exxon Shipping
Type of Crime: Environmental
Criminal Fine: $125 million

6) UCAR International, Inc.
Type of Crime: Antitrust
Criminal Fine: $110 million

7) Archer Daniels Midland
Type of Crime: Antitrust
Criminal Fine: $100 million

8)(tie) Banker's Trust
Type of Crime: Financial
Criminal Fine: $60 million

8)(tie) Sears Bankruptcy Recovery Management Services
Type of Crime: Fraud
Criminal Fine: $60 million

10) Haarman & Reimer Corp.
Type of Crime: Antitrust
Criminal Fine: $50 million

11) Louisiana-Pacific Corporation
Type of Crime: Environmental
Criminal Fine: $37 million

12) Hoechst AG

Type of Crime: Antitrust
Criminal Fine: $36 million
13) **Damon Clinical Laboratories, Inc.**
Type of Crime: Fraud
Criminal Fine: $35.2 million
14) **C.R. Bard Inc.**
Type of Crime: Food and drug
Criminal Fine: $30.9 million 7
15) **Genentech Inc.**
Type of Crime: Food and drug
Criminal Fine: $30 million
16) **Nippon Gohsei**
Type of Crime: Antitrust
Criminal Fine: $21 million
17)(tie) **Pfizer Inc.**
Type of Crime: Antitrust
Criminal Fine: $20 million
17)(tie) **Summitville Consolidated Mining Co. Inc.**
Type of Crime: Environmental
Criminal Fine: $20 million 10
19)(tie) **Lucas Western Inc.**
Type of Crime: False Statements
Criminal Fine: $18.5 million 9
19)(tie) **Rockwell International Corporation**
Type of Crime: Environmental
Criminal Fine: $18.5 million
21) **Royal Caribbean Cruises Ltd.**
Type of Crime: Environmental
Criminal Fine: $18 million
22) **Teledyne Industries Inc.**
Type of Crime: Fraud
Criminal Fine: $17.5 million
23) **Northrop**
Type of Crime: False statements
Criminal Fine: $17 million

24) **Litton Applied Technology Division (ATD) and Litton Systems Canada (LSL)**
Type of Crime: Fraud
Criminal Fine: $16.5 million
25) **Iroquois Pipeline Operating Company**
Type of Crime: Environmental
Criminal Fine: $15 million
26) **Eastman Chemical Company**
Type of Crime: Antitrust
Criminal Fine: $11 million
27) **Copley Pharmaceutical, Inc.**
Type of Crime: Food and drug
Criminal Fine: $10.65 million
28) **Lonza AG**
Type of Crime: Antitrust
Criminal Fine: $10.5 million
29) **Kimberly Home Health Care Inc.**
Type of Crime: Fraud
Criminal Fine: $10.08 million
30)(tie) **Ajinomoto Co. Inc.**
Type of Crime: Antitrust
Criminal Fine: $10 million
30)(tie) **Bank of Credit and Commerce International (BCCI)**
Type of Crime: Financial
Criminal Fine: $10 million
30)(tie) **Kyowa Hakko Kogyo Co. Ltd.**
Type of Crime: Antitrust
Criminal Fine: $10 million
30)(tie) **Warner-Lambert Company**
Type of Crime: Food and drug
Criminal Fine: $10 million
34) **General Electric**
Type of Crime: Fraud
Criminal Fine: $9.5 million
35)(tie) **Royal Caribbean Cruises Ltd.**

Type of Crime: Environmental
Criminal Fine: $9 million
35)(tie) **Showa Denko Carbon**
Type of Crime: Antitrust
Criminal Fine: $9 million
37) **IBM East Europe/Asia Ltd.**
Type of Crime: Illegal exports
Criminal Fine: $8.5 million
38) **Empire Sanitary Landfill Inc.**
Type of crime: Campaign finance
Criminal Fine: $8 million
39)(tie) **Colonial Pipeline Company**
Type of Crime: Environmental
Criminal Fine: $7 million
39)(tie) **Eklof Marine Corporation**
Type of Crime: Environmental
Criminal Fine: $7 million
41)(tie) **Chevron**
Type of Crime: Environmental
Criminal Fine: $6.5 million
41)(tie) **Rockwell International Corporation**
Type of Crime: Environmental
Criminal Fine: $6.5 million
43) **Tokai Carbon Ltd. Co.**
Type of Crime: Antitrust
Criminal Fine: $6 million
44)(tie) **Allied Clinical Laboratories, Inc.**
Type of Crime: Fraud
Criminal Fine: $5 million
44)(tie) **Northern Brands International Inc.**
Type of Crime: Fraud
Criminal Fine: $5 million
44)(tie) **Ortho Pharmaceutical Corporation**
Type of Crime: Obstruction of justice
Criminal Fine: $5 million

44)(tie) Unisys
Type of Crime: Bribery
Criminal Fine: $5 million
44)(tie) Georgia Pacific Corporation
Type of Crime: Tax evasion
Criminal Fine: $5 million 5
49) Kanzaki Specialty Papers Inc.
Type of Crime: Antitrust
Criminal Fine: $4.5 million
50) ConAgra Inc.
Type of Crime: Fraud
Criminal Fine: $4.4 million
51) Ryland Mortgage Company
Type of Crime: Financial
Criminal Fine: $4.2 million
52)(tie) Blue Cross Blue Shield of Illinois
Type of Crime: Fraud
Criminal Fine: $4 million
52)(tie) Borden Inc.
Type of Crime: Antitrust
Criminal Fine: $4 million
52)(tie) Dexter Corporation
Type of Crime: Environmental
Criminal Fine: $4 million
52)(tie) Southland Corporation
Type of Crime: Antitrust
Criminal Fine: $4 million
52)(tie) Teledyne Industries Inc.
Type of Crime: Illegal exports
Criminal Fine: $4 million
52)(tie) Tyson Foods Inc.
Type of Crime: Public corruption
Criminal Fine: $4 million
58)(tie) Aluminum Company of America (ALCOA)
Type of Crime: Environmental

Criminal Fine: $3.75 million
58)(tie) **Costain Coal Inc.**
Type of Crime: Worker Death
Criminal Fine: $3.75 million
58)(tie) **United States Sugar Corporation**
Type of Crime: Environmental
Criminal Fine: $3.75 million
61) **Saybolt, Inc., Saybolt North America**
Type of Crime: Environmental, bribery
Criminal Fine: $3.4 million
62)(tie) **Bristol-Myers Squibb**
Type of Crime: Environmental
Criminal Fine: $3 million
62)(tie) **Chemical Waste Management Inc.**
Type of Crime: Environmental
Criminal Fine: $3 million
62)(tie) **Ketchikan Pulp Company**
Type of Crime: Environmental
Criminal Fine: $3 million
62)(tie) **United Technologies Corporation**
Type of Crime: Environmental
Criminal Fine: $3 million
62)(tie) **Warner-Lambert Inc.**
Type of Crime: Environmental
Criminal Fine: $3 million
67)(tie) **Arizona Chemical Co. Inc.**
Type of Crime: Environmental
Criminal Fine: $2.5 million
67)(tie) **Consolidated Rail Corporation (Conrail)**
Type of Crime: Environmental
Criminal Fine: $2.5 million
69) **International Paper**
Type of Crime: Environmental
Criminal Fine: $2.2 million
70)(tie) **Consolidated Edison Company**

Type of Crime: Environmental
Criminal Fine: $2 million
70)(tie) **Crop Growers Corporation**
Type of Crime: Campaign finance
Criminal Fine: $2 million
70)(tie) **E-Systems Inc.**
Type of Crime: Fraud
Criminal Fine: $2 million
70)(tie) **HAL Beheer BV**
Type of Crime: Environmental
Criminal Fine: $2 million
70)(tie) **John Morrell and Company**
Type of Crime: Environmental
Criminal Fine: $2 million
70)(tie) **United Technologies Corporation**
Type of Crime: Fraud
Criminal Fine: $2 million
76) **Mitsubishi Corporation, Mitsubishi International Corporation**
Type of Crime: Antitrust
Criminal Fine: $1.8 million
77)(tie) **Blue Shield of California**
Type of Crime: Fraud
Criminal Fine: $1.5 million
77)(tie) **Browning-Ferris Inc.**
Type of Crime: Environmental
Criminal Fine: $1.5 million
77)(tie) **Odwalla Inc.**
Type of Crime: Food and drug
Criminal Fine: $1.5 million
77)(tie) **Teledyne Inc.**
Type of Crime: False statements
Criminal Fine: $1.5 million
77)(tie) **Unocal Corporation**
Type of Crime: Environmental

Criminal Fine: $1.5 million
82)(tie) **Doyon Drilling Inc.**
Type of Crime: Environmental
Criminal Fine: $1 million
82)(tie) **Eastman Kodak**
Type of Crime: Environmental
Criminal Fine: $1 million
82)(tie) **Case Corporation**
Type of Crime: Illegal exports
Criminal Fine: $1 million
85) **Marathon Oil**
Type of Crime: Environmental
Criminal Fine: $900,000
86) **Hyundai Motor Company**
Type of Crime: Campaign finance
Criminal Fine: $600,000
87)(tie) **Baxter International Inc.**
Type of Crime: Illegal Boycott
Criminal Fine: $500,000
87)(tie) **Bethship-Sabine Yard**
Type of Crime: Environmental
Criminal Fine: $500,000
87(tie) **Palm Beach Cruises**
Type of Crime: Environmental
Criminal Fine: $500,000
87)(tie) **Princess Cruises Inc.**
Type of Crime: Environmental
Criminal Fine: $500,000
91)(tie) **Cerestar Bioproducts BV**
Type of Crime: Antitrust
Criminal Fine: $400,000
91)(tie) **Sun-Land Products of California**
Type of Crime: Campaign finance
Criminal Fine: $400,000
93)(tie) **American Cyanamid**

Type of Crime: Environmental
Criminal Fine: $250,000
93)(tie) **Korean Air Lines**
Type of Crime: Campaign finance
Criminal Fine: $250,000
93)(tie) **Regency Cruises Inc.**
Type of Crime: Environmental
Criminal Fine: $250,000
96)(tie) **Adolph Coors Company**
Type of Crime: Environmental
Criminal Fine: $200,000
96)(tie) **Andrew and Williamson Sales Co.**
Type of crime: Food and drug
Criminal Fine: $200,000
96)(tie) **Daewoo International (America) Corporation**
Type of Fine: Campaign finance
Criminal Fine: $200,000
96)(tie) **Exxon Corporation**
Type of Crime: Environmental
Criminal Fine: $200,000
100) **Samsung America Inc.**
Type of Crime: Campaign finance
Criminal Fine: $150,000

PART NINE
RESISTANCE

For all the amassed power of Big Business, it has never been the case that a docile citizenry has uniformly accepted the corporate hegemonic project.

Communities across the United States, and the world, have resisted efforts to use their lands for garbage dumps, to rip out their natural resources without due compensation or respect for the environment, to gouge them in the provision of essential goods and services. Workers have stood up to demands for givebacks, strikebreaking and unionbusting schemes, and management efforts to skirt safe practices. In some countries, popular movements have contested for, and occasionally won, political power. Global solidarity campaigns have supported citizen movements in flashpoint conflicts: sweatshop workers in Indonesia or Nicaragua, producing for companies like Nike, Wal-mart and Kohl's, indigenous groups in the Amazon resisting encroachment on the forest, a Bolivian town resisting a water privatization scheme designed by Bechtel and the World Bank, health workers in poor countries trying to deliver essential medicines to sick people, U.S. workers striking against UPS, French farmers who refuse to allow McDonald's and the corporate food industry to homogenize the world's food supply.

But always the issue is the scope of the resistance, and its level of organization.

The November-December 1999 protests in Seattle against the World Trade Organization appears to have ushered in a new and impressive worldwide level of resistance. Seattle was followed by an April 2000 demonstration against the IMF and World Bank in Washington, D.C., protests at the Republican and Democratic conventions, a September 2000 mobilization in Melbourne against the World Business Forum, the September 2000 protests in Prague at the IMF/World Bank annual meetings, plus many similar, mobilizations.

The protests were colorful, creative, dynamic and filled with youthful enthusiasm and energy. They seem the manifestation of a growing rejection of a corporatized economy, politics and culture.

The future of the disparate movement against corporate power is unsure. Some campaigns waned, even as a timely global movement against the U.S. war on Iraq startled the militarists in Washington, London, Madrid, Rome and elsewhere.

Does the citizen upsurge have the staying power and cohesiveness to go beyond street protests and campaigns against particular business abuses? Certainly, it has a long way to go before reversing the corporate stranglehold over society. But it our best hope to rescue our lives, and our planet, from the corporate grip.

The Committee of the Sheets

March 23, 1999

The Mayor of Palermo, Sicily, Leoluca Orlando, was in Washington, D.C. the other day, telling reporters how the citizens of his fair city led a cultural revolt against the Mafia. Make no mistake, the Mayor cautioned, the Mafia still had its grips on some of the city's businesses, but the Mafia no longer dominates Palermo's institutions.

After especially brutal Mafia executions of two Sicilian judges, one citizen scrawled anti-mafia signs on a bedsheet and hung it from her window. Then others joined in. The "Committee of the Sheets" was formed.

The bedsheet protest caught on until the vast majority of city residents were hanging bedsheets.

"On certain days, you could look up at an apartment building and see where the Mafia don lived—it was the apartment without a bedsheet hanging from its window," the Mayor told reporters.

The bedsheet protest was followed by marches, sit-ins, demonstrations. The populists didn't let up until the Mafia's grip on the city was broken.

Orlando was touring the United States earlier this month, inviting fellow activists and reporters to come to Palermo in June to attend a conference on democracy and the rule of law.

We asked Orlando whether lessons from Palermo's fight against the Mafia's grip on Sicily could be applied to break the grip of corporations in the United States. He cracked a little smile, then begged off, muttering something about not wanting to interfere in the internal affairs of a foreign country.

But we believe the lessons are applicable.

After all, 100 years ago, the citizenry viewed corporations as soulless, amoral, sometimes evil conglomerations of capital.

As Roland Marchand, the late University of California Davis Professor of American History, makes clear in *Creating the*

Corporate Soul: The Rise of Public Relations and Corporate Imagery in American Big Business (University of California Press, 1998), for all the legal legitimacy that the courts bestowed upon corporations at the turn of the century, corporations "conspicuously lacked a comparable social and moral legitimacy in the eyes of the public."

"The big business corporation, as a rising chorus of American voices chanted insistently from the 1890s onward, had no soul," Marchand writes.

The corporation had no soul, it had no conscience, and was driven by a bottom line profit urgency that often trampled on the rights of living, breathing persons.

"If some of the great entrepreneurs of the 1870s and 1880s had proved greedy and ruthless in their pursuit of profits, the new corporations of the 1890s and 1900s would have even fewer scruples," Marchand writes. "After all, one might appeal to the conscience of an individual businessman. But the soulless corporation, driven by a cold economic logic that defined its every decision as a money equation, had none."

Big Business realized that this public perception of the corporation as a cold, impersonal "thing" would hinder its domination of the political economy. So big corporations launched a 100-year public relations campaign to "create the corporate soul"—to convince Americans that corporations had a moral purpose and were serving the public good.

And it is clear today, to all but the most conflicted observers, that the campaign Marchand documents in his book has succeeded beyond the wildest dreams of its creators.

Marchand amassed copies of thousands of corporate image ads, many of which illustrate *Creating the Corporate Soul*. In a chapter on AT&T, Marchand reprints a turn-of-the-century ad titled "Democracy: of the people, by the people, for the people" showing workers who are shareholders of AT&T. A similar AT&T ad from 1919 titled "Our Stockholders" shows a mother surrounded by two young sons perusing her stock certificates.

Marchand dryly notes: "No plutocrats were visible here."

Today, the corporate hucksters have taken their public relations campaign to a laughable extreme, portraying, for example, corporations not just as friendly beings, but as friends of workers—even as revolutionaries.

As cultural historian Thomas Frank points out, Pizza Hut has a television commercial that sympathizes with labor organizers. According to Frank, the ad, titled "Strike Break," juxtaposes a group of "angry workers stomping around outside a factory with a group of generically concerned executives inside the building."

A truck pulls up and delivers pizza to the striking workers, "who drop their picket signs and smile gratefully at the white-collar figures looking down on them from above."

"And so, thanks to the management team, a century of labor struggle has been swept away," Frank concludes. "The world of business is the world, period. There's nothing outside of it. Get as mad as you want—the pizza trucks are standing by."

In the face of this corporate onslaught, some may want to throw in the towel. We'd rather reach for the bedsheet.

Why Bother?

November 5, 1999

We have been writing this column for a couple of years now. Periodically, we'll get a message from a reader that goes something like this:

"I've been reading your column for a while, but it's all negative. You lay out the problems—problem after problem, week after week—but give no hint at a solution. It's all so depressing. Please take me off your list."

We and others can advocate more democracy until we turn blue in the face, but at some point, we must look carefully at the question of why, given the facts on the ground, there is no mass human revolt against the corporate control over our democracy.

We set out recently in search of solutions. And luckily for us, our first stop was the Washington, D.C. office of the Sam Smith.

Smith is the editor of Progressive Review, and is a long-time small d democrat. Smith has written a new book, tentatively titled: *Why Bother? Reasons for Doing and Being.* He's searching for a publisher.

Smith says that during a meeting on a new journalistic enterprise in the 1980s, he realized that to a large degree, facts didn't matter anymore. "I noticed that truth was no longer setting people free," he writes, "it was only making them drowsy."

We were in an age, as philosophy professor Rick Roderick put it, where everything once directly lived was being turned into a representation of itself.

So, Roderick argued, we watched Michael Jordan to remember what a life filled with physical exertion was about. Similarly, Smith says, we now watch C-SPAN, to remember what democracy was about.

As we were glued to the television set and computer screen, a culture of impunity took hold.

How does a culture of impunity differ from ordinary political corruption?

Ordinary political corruption represents the corruption of the culture. A culture of impunity becomes the culture.

"Such a culture does not announce itself," writes Smith. "It creeps up, day by day, deal by deal, euphemism by euphemism. The intellectual achievement, technocratic pyrotechnics and calm rationality that serves as a patina for the culture of impunity can be dangerously misleading. In a culture of impunity, what replaces constitution, precedent, values, tradition, fairness, consensus, debate, and all that sort of arcane stuff? Mainly greed."

Smith reminds us that the Italians, who invented the term fascism, also called it estato corporativo—the corporatist state.

"Orwell rightly described fascism as being an extension of capitalism," Smith writes. "It is an economy in which the government serves the interests of the oligopolies, a state in which large corporations have the powers that in a democracy devolve to the citizen."

Is there any doubt that ours is a corporate state?

No.

And it is our increased consciousness of the corporate state that has led us to deeper despair.

"To accept the full consequences of the degradation of the environment, the explosion of incarceration, the creeping militarization, the dismantling of democracy, the commodification of culture, the contempt for the real, the culture of impunity among the powerful and zero tolerance towards the weak, requires a courage that seems beyond us," Smith writes. "We do not know how to look honestly at the wreckage without an overwhelming sense of surrender."

In the face of this despair, Smith rejects the way of the reformer in the hope that a new activism will arise—the citizen who will seek the "hat trick of integrity, passion and rebellion."

"We need no more town meetings, no more expertise, no

more public interest activists playing technocratic chess with government bureaucrats, no more changes in paragraph 324B of an ineffectual law, no more talking heads," he writes.

Instead, we need an uprising of the soul, that spirit of which Aldous Huxley described as "irrelevant, irreverent, out of key with all that has gone before."

Smith wants to see Huxley's uprising of the soul. He's asking us to begin to fundamentally question the corporate culture that has, step by step, unannounced, engulfed us—junk food pushers in the schools, tort deformers educating judges, oil companies cleaning up in public museums, big companies of all stripes taking over public interest groups—the list is endless.

The uprising of the soul will replace the reformer with the rebel, the negotiator with the defender of justice, the prevaricator with the honest citizen, the diplomat with the radical.

"We need to think the unthinkable even when the possible is undoable, the ideal is unimaginable, when power overwhelms truth, when compulsion replaces choice," Smith writes. "We need to lift our eyes from the bottom lines to the hills, from the screen to the sky, from the adjacent to the hazy horizon."

Why bother? Smith asks.

We have no other choice.

A Whiff of Democracy in Seattle

December 6, 1999

Democracy was certainly in the streets of Seattle last week, and a whiff—perhaps carried by teargas—even made it into the convention center where trade ministers from the World Trade Organization (WTO) member states met.

Many factors contributed to the collapse of the WTO talks—an effort to expand the scope of the trade agency's authority—but there is no question that popular protests played a central role.

Tuesday saw at least 40,000 people take to the streets to protest the corporate tilt of the WTO. A stunning coalition of teamsters, consumers, sea turtle protection activists, religious people, women's groups, environmentalists, students and anti-corporate youth and many, many others joined to "Just Say No to the WTO."

Approximately 10,000 people—primarily students and youth—joined together in an extraordinarily well organized and highly disciplined direct action to block every access way to the convention center, stopping most of the official and negotiating activities scheduled for the WTO meeting's first working day.

Notwithstanding city efforts to clamp down on all public dissent in the downtown area, protests continued throughout the week, with thousands demonstrating at separate environmental, farmer, steel worker and women's marches and rallies. Always on display were focused attacks on the WTO and strident criticism of the corporations that have drafted and lobbied for its anti-people rules.

On Friday, perhaps ten thousand joined in a labor-led march—organized on about 24 hours notice—to again protest the WTO and the city's infringements on civil liberties through the creation of a "no protest" zone.

Meanwhile, students and others in an overwhelmingly

young crowd continued civil disobedience and direct actions throughout the week.

Inside the convention center, where negotiations began on Wednesday after riot-gear-equipped police and national guard forces cordoned off the downtown from most protesters, turmoil was building as well.

When separate working groups negotiating over a wide array of sectors failed to produce compromise agreements, the United States sought to forge a deal through the WTO's heavy-handed old-style tactics.

Charlene Barshefsky, the U.S. Trade Representative, and the rest of the U.S. negotiating team picked a handful of countries to commence negotiations in a closed "Green Room." The idea was for the arbitrarily selected bunch to work out a comprehensive deal, and then present it to the entire WTO membership as a fait accompli for adoption. But even the Green Room gambit failed, and the talks ended in complete disarray.

The complexity of trade negotiations—with compromises made in one sector dependent on unrelated compromises in another—means no single factor can explain the talks' failure. But it is possible to identify many of the key negotiating reasons for the collapse:

* The European Union and the United States could not work out an agricultural accommodation, with the EU's commitment to export subsidies a critical stumbling block.

* Many Third World countries revolted against the negotiating process, and their complete exclusion from the Green Room discussions. More than 70 developing countries, primarily from Africa and the Caribbean, declared on Thursday that they would not sign a final declaration negotiated in a process from which they had been excluded.

* Many Third World countries resisted the U.S. call for formation of a working group to study the relationship between trade and labor issues.

* A compromise deal that was floated early Friday morn-

ing would have entailed politically unacceptable compromises on the key issues of concern to U.S. labor unions—anti-dumping (rules permitting countries to block the import of below-market-cost imports) and some progress on rules to promote adherence to core labor standards.

On each of these issues, the street protests helped heighten contradictions and conflicts. The simple fact of preventing negotiations on Tuesday helped impede agreement in the agricultural sector. As a delegate from Zimbabwe explained, the street demonstrations emboldened the Third World negotiators to object to the exclusionary processes inside the WTO. And the demands from the U.S. labor movement—backed by mobilized rank-and-file members—stiffened the U.S. negotiators so that they at least refused to cave in on their minimalist labor rights demands.

For now, street heat has stifled the corporate elite. Just as they blocked delegates from entering the convention center, so they blocked the corporations' attempt to extend the WTO's reach even further into nation's economies and societies.

But as spectacular as was the Seattle victory, achieving the second half of one of the week's primary slogans—"No New Round, Turnaround"—will be even more daunting. Launching a new WTO negotiating round is nowhere near as important to corporate interests as maintaining existing WTO rules and the prevailing model of corporate globalization.

Still, a little bit of democratic empowerment can be a dangerous thing. If the broad coalition that came together in Seattle can stay together—a big "if"—it may eventually be able to force new rules for the global economy, so that trade is finally subordinated to the humane values of health, safety, ecological sustainability and respect for human rights, rather than the reverse.

The Meaning of April 16

April 19, 2000

The April 16 protests in Washington, D.C. against the International Monetary Fund (IMF) and World Bank made history and marked a new phase in the effort to halt and reverse the processes of corporate globalization.

Citizens in developing countries—from Jordan to Zambia, Indonesia to Venezuela—have long protested against the policies of the IMF and World Bank. On April 16, for the first time, citizens in the United States came out in large numbers to join the calls for a rollback of IMF and World Bank powers.

Tens of thousands of people took to the streets, or joined a permitted demonstration on the Ellipse to denounce structural adjustment policies—the deregulatory policy package that the Fund and Bank impose on country after country—for hurting the poor and exacerbating economic inequality.

The exact impact of the demonstrations will only be apparent in the years to come, but it is already clear that the protests—evidence of the deepening citizen movement against corporate globalization—have had dramatic effect.

First, the U.S. public is newly aware of what the IMF and World Bank are, and millions of people in the United States have for the first time learned of how the institutions' policies hurt people in poor countries.

In anticipation of the protests, the mainstream media focused some attention on structural adjustment policies, both by conveying the viewpoints of the Mobilization for Global Justice and, in some instances, by actually reporting on the effects of structural adjustment in countries like Haiti or Tanzania. There was probably more U.S. mainstream media coverage of IMF/World Bank/structural adjustment issues in the past two weeks than in the previous 20 years combined.

The growing U.S. public concern with IMF and World Bank policy is crucial because while the Fund and Bank are unaccountable to the people in the Third World they are allegedly trying to help, they are responsive to the United States—the largest shareholder in both institutions and the dominant influence at the IMF in particular.

The second noteworthy outcome from the April 16 protests was the role of U.S. organized labor in the permitted demonstration on the Ellipse. The AFL-CIO and a number of major unions, including the Service Employees, the Teamsters, the Steelworkers, the American Federation of Government Employees, the United Electrical workers and UNITE, the textile union, endorsed the demonstration, and many of the unions sent top officials to address the rally.

Two years ago, the AFL-CIO lent its support to the Clinton administration's request for $18 billion in funding for the IMF, so the newfound willingness to strongly denounce IMF and Bank structural adjustment policies represents an important shift.

The AFL-CIO is also beginning to develop a penetrating critique of the notion of export-led development—one of the core principles of structural adjustment. Instead of joining in a race to the bottom to produce goods using sweatshop labor or lax environmental standards, the AFL-CIO is suggesting, countries should instead concentrate on developing productive capacity to meet local needs.

A third historic occurrence was the endorsement by members of the G-77—a grouping of most of the world's developing nations—of the Washington protests and a stinging condemnation of the Fund and Bank's structural adjustment policies.

"I, for one, support the demonstrators," said Arthur Mbanefo of Nigeria, spokesperson for the G-77 during its recent three-day summit in Havana. "Many countries have rejected the results of various policy initiatives of the World Bank and IMF," he said, citing privatization, a refusal to cancel debt and a "one-size-fits-all" structural adjustment agenda. "We are very supportive of demonstrations that could forcefully handle those concerns."

The DC protests seem to have exerted a "Columbus Effect." Just as the Columbus, Ohio protests against Clinton administration plans to bomb Iraq led Egyptian President Mubarak to comment that surely he could oppose bombing if the people of Columbus did, so the Washington protests against the IMF and World Bank have created more political space for developing countries to speak up on behalf of their own interests.

The IMF and World Bank spokespeople acknowledged the protests—pointing out that it was impossible to ignore them. They emphasized that they are increasingly focusing on poverty and trying to empower the poor. But they refuse to abandon their emphasis on structural adjustment, and in fact are using their very modest debt relief initiative to force poor countries to undergo still more, carefully monitored structural adjustment.

Real change at the IMF and World Bank will come not from voluntary "reforms" in their policies, but from external forces—such as the U.S. Congress or large numbers of developing country governments cooperating closely—that demand that IMF and Bank powers be curtailed.

With the April 16 protests shining light on the policies of the IMF and World Bank, expanding the coalition opposed to structural adjustment and revealing that discontent in the developing world with IMF and Bank policies is increasingly matched by similar outrage in the rich nations, the prospect of a successful drive to shrink the authority and power of the IMF and Bank is greater than at any time in recent history.

Shredded: Justice Delivered to BAT

April 23, 2002

The latest evidence that Enron and Arthur Andersen are not aberrations comes from Australia.

There, a judge has concluded that British American Tobacco (BAT) has engaged in a massive document-destruction scheme intentionally designed to thwart smokers or former smokers from bringing suit against the company.

The judge found the document destruction to be so serious that he directed a verdict for the plaintiff in the case before him, a 51-year-old Australian woman named Rolah Ann McCabe, without permitting BAT to mount a defense.

In a 133-page decision issued in March but just recently made public, Judge Geoffrey Eames details an elaborate, carefully considered, company-wide document-destruction scheme

"The predominant purpose of the document destruction," the judge found, "was the denial to plaintiffs of information which was likely to be of importance in proving their case, in particular, proving the state of knowledge of the defendant of the health risks of smoking, the addictive qualities of cigarettes and the response of the defendant to such knowledge."

The company was a defendant in various lawsuits from 1990 until 1998, during which time shredding may have stopped, though the judge expresses skepticism about this claim.

In February 1996, Phyllis Cremona brought suit against BAT in Australian courts. In the course of the discovery phase of that litigation, BAT's subsidiary identified 30,000 documents as possibly relevant to the proceeding. With a few exceptions, BAT scanned all of the documents, creating electronic versions. Company lawyers also indexed and summarized virtually all of the documents. The lawyers rated each document on a scale of one to five, according to how damaging each was likely to be to the company in litigation. A rating of five meant the document was a "knockout" against the company, a rating of one a "knockout" for BAT.

Only about 200 of the documents were requested by the plaintiff in the Cremona case.

When the Cremona case ended and with no pending litigation, BAT's chief counsel told an associate, "now is a good opportunity to dispose of documents if we no longer need to keep them. That should be done outside the legal department."

Thousands of the 30,000 documents were then destroyed. Also destroyed were the electronic versions of the documents, the summaries, indices and ratings.

"The decision to destroy all such lists and records," the judge concluded, "can only have been a deliberate tactic designed to hide information as to what was destroyed."

In 2001, the McCabe litigation commenced. In the course of discovery, the plaintiff's lawyers requested a range of materials which it appears would have included many of the documents in the Cremona database, but were destroyed after that case's completion.

Rather than acknowledge the destruction of the documents, however, BAT lawyers engaged in a series of obfuscations and delaying tactics. The judge found that the BAT lawyers misled both the court and the plaintiff's lawyers, though eventually through persistent questioning the document-destruction scheme was revealed.

BAT defended, and continues to defend, the shredding on the grounds that the company was not obligated to hold on to documents that may be useful to an opposing party in some future litigation. With no litigation pending after the Cremona case, document destruction was proper, the company claims.

But the judge stated that while corporations are not obligated to store documents indefinitely, they are not free to destroy them in anticipation of future litigation. In BAT's case, the company and its lawyers viewed future litigation as a "virtual certainty," the judge held. "At all times those who took the decisions about the implementation of the policy regarded future proceedings to be not merely likely, but to be a near certainty," Judge Eames wrote. "It was that certainty which meant that any opportunity to destroy documents which arose by virtue of the elimination of current proceedings was to be seized upon."

The judge concluded that the exact prejudicial effect to McCabe was unknowable—since "the prejudice to the plaintiff might be immense by virtue of the deliberate destruction of one document, which might have been decisive in her case"—but potentially extreme. Accordingly, the judge issued a ruling in favor of McCabe, without permitting BAT to mount a defense.

A jury issued an award of more than $350,000. With their client likely to die at any time, McCabe's lawyers had agreed before trial that no punitive damages would be sought, in order to expedite the trial.

BAT has said it will appeal the judge's decision.

The potential implication of the decision is enormous. While Judge Eames' decision will have no binding effect in future cases, other judges, confronted with the same evidentiary problems as in the McCabe case, are likely to consider following Eames' example. BAT may find itself in Australia facing the flood of litigation it long feared, but without the ability to defend itself.

The decision also has potential implications in the United States, especially because Judge Eames' findings are that U.S. lawyers for BAT—both company counsel and the Kansas City tobacco firm of Shook Hardy and Bacon—played a critical role in directing the document destruction.

Move over Ken Lay, Jeffrey Skilling and David Duncan of Arthur Andersen. You have company.

Militarization in Miami: Threatening the Right to Protest

November 26, 2003

There was a real threat to the social order on the streets of Miami last week, during the Ministerial Meeting of the Free Trade Area of the Americas (FTAA).

It wasn't protesters, not even those calling themselves anarchists or even those dressed in black.

No, the threat came from the Miami police, Florida state troopers and the other police and military forces patrolling the city.

With more than $10 million in special funding (including an $8.5 million allocation in the federal government's Iraq appropriations bill), 2,500 or so officers—many clad in full body armor and backed up by armored vehicles—turned Miami into a veritable police state.

As was almost inevitable, the police used wildly excessive force to deal with protesters. They launched unprovoked attacks against people who were doing nothing illegal. They sprayed tear gas and pepper spray at protesters—including retirees—and shot many with rubber bullets. They used taser guns. They knocked down peaceful protesters and held guns to their heads. They blocked thousands of retirees and union members on buses from joining a rally and march for which all required permits had been obtained. They attacked journalists viewed as hostile. They arrested approximately 250 persons, according to the best estimates, with little or no rationale. Credible reports have emerged of brutality and sexual harassment against several of those jailed.

At least as serious, the police deterred thousands from even considering joining the FTAA protests—and protests into the future.

In sunny Miami, it was a dark week for the First Amendment, for civil liberties and for the right to dissent.

A South African activist told us how deeply frightened she was walking down the streets of Miami. Even before the police violence erupted, marching in the streets amidst thousands of armored police sent chills down her spine, she said.

Last week's outrages had their roots in months of planning led by Miami Police Chief John Timoney. He whipped the city and the police force into a frenzy. The absurdist invocation of an anarchist threat convinced the local media (especially television reporters) and much of the local population that downtown would be a riot zone. That was enough to empty the downtown, and scare many local Miamians from joining any of the protests, no matter how tame.

We had first-hand experience with this problem. We had been involved in a planning a small demonstration on Tuesday—two days before the main protests. We had obtained all requisite permits from the police. With agreement from their schools, more than 100 high school students were eager to join our small action highlighting how the FTAA and trade agreements interfere with anti-smoking and other public health measures. But no school could feel comfortable sending students to a militarized downtown, and so the students were not able to demonstrate. We turned our rally into a news conference.

This was a small incident. Our demonstration wasn't going to change the world. (We do, however, intend to win on our demand to exclude tobacco products from all trade agreements.) But as an illustrative example, it is incredibly important, for it shows how police overdeployment, scare tactics and militarization intimidates people from marching in the streets and opposing corporate- and state-approved policy.

It wasn't just the public and media that Timoney managed to frighten. There's little doubt that the police themselves buy the propaganda. After months of excessive training and hearing about the dangers posed by protesters, and empowered by new body armor, shields, batons and other equipment, the police were, to say the least, overeager to lunge at protesters. (Said one of a group of 10 cops on bikes as they crossed the street to assess the scene at our news conference, and with one of us standing right next to them, "Let's go fuck 'em up.")

By the time of the main demonstrations on Thursday, the police couldn't hold themselves back.

In different circumstances, it would have been funny to see the police outnumbering the direct action protesters, or the comically attired "undercover" agents who were a bit too well built to credibly seem part of the ranks of the slight direct action protesters—many of whom are vegans.

But it wasn't funny.

Not when the police—responding to the smallest provocations, such as a couple small fires lit in trashcans—went berserk and attacked large crowds of protesters. Not when credible reports say some of those undercover agents may have been provocateurs, and when several of them emerged as some of the most brutal in attacking protesters.

There is immediate need now to support those who were jailed and mistreated, and force the city to drop trumped up charges against protesters.

You can help by sending a fax to Miami Mayor Manuel Diaz protesting the violation of constitutional rights.

Those who are facing charges will need legal help.

Activists, the National Lawyers Guild, the American Civil Liberties Union and other civil liberties standard bearers must do all they can and will do to oppose the rising repression evidenced in Miami. But that's not enough.

There will, undoubtedly, be civil lawsuits down the road, and, if there is any justice, they will succeed. But that's not enough, either. As important as such litigation is, it is clear from recent crackdown on protests around the United States that police forces are willing to absorb the costs of these suits.

The present cycle is that the media and political establishment applaud the police for running scare campaigns, militarizing cities, directing violence against protesters and blatantly violating civil liberties. Often, as details emerge, criticism emerges from those same pillars of society.

This must change. The establishment must speak out now, immediately after the abuses occurred. They are apparent to anyone who cares to know about them.

In the future, the establishment—we mean newspaper editors, political leaders of all parties, lawyers, even corporate executives—must insist on appropriate police tactics in advance of large-scale protests, and they must make clear that regular police and top officers alike will be held personally accountable for abuses. If they fail to pursue this course, the consequences for the right to protest will be grim indeed.

About the Authors

Russell Mokhiber is editor of *Corporate Crime Reporter*, a legal weekly based in Washington, DC. He is also author of *Corporate Crime and Violence*.

Robert Weissman is editor of the Washington DC-based *Multinational Monitor*, the leading source of critical reporting on corporate power. He is also co-director of Essential Action, a corporate accountability group.

Mokhiber and Weissman are co-authors of *Corporate Predators: The Hunt for Mega-Profits and the Attack on Democracy*.

For More Great Info

On The Rampage is a compendium of the "Focus on the Corporation" column written by Russell Mokhiber and Robert Weissman. If you would like to receive a free electronic subscription to the column, go to
<http://litss.essential.org/mailman/listinfo/corp-focus> or send an email message to corp-focus-admin@lists.essential.org with the subject line "subscribe."

Subscriptions to *Multinational Monitor* magaizne are available for $29.95/year from:

Multinational Monitor
P.O. Box 19405
Washington, DC 20036
Tel: 202-387-8030
Fax: 202-234-5176
Email: monitor@essential.org

Or, visit the *Multinational Monitor* website,
<www.multinationalmonitor.org>.